1,000,000 Books
are available to read at

Forgotten Books

www.ForgottenBooks.com

Read online
Download PDF
Purchase in print

ISBN 978-1-330-42566-4
PIBN 10061089

This book is a reproduction of an important historical work. Forgotten Books uses state-of-the-art technology to digitally reconstruct the work, preserving the original format whilst repairing imperfections present in the aged copy. In rare cases, an imperfection in the original, such as a blemish or missing page, may be replicated in our edition. We do, however, repair the vast majority of imperfections successfully; any imperfections that remain are intentionally left to preserve the state of such historical works.

Forgotten Books is a registered trademark of FB &c Ltd.
Copyright © 2018 FB &c Ltd.
FB &c Ltd, Dalton House, 60 Windsor Avenue, London, SW19 2RR.
Company number 08720141. Registered in England and Wales.

For support please visit www.forgottenbooks.com

1 MONTH OF FREE READING

at

www.ForgottenBooks.com

By purchasing this book you are eligible for one month membership to ForgottenBooks.com, giving you unlimited access to our entire collection of over 1,000,000 titles via our web site and mobile apps.

To claim your free month visit:

www.forgottenbooks.com/free61089

* Offer is valid for 45 days from date of purchase. Terms and conditions apply.

English
Français
Deutsche
Italiano
Español
Português

www.forgottenbooks.com

Mythology Photography **Fiction**
Fishing Christianity **Art** Cooking
Essays Buddhism Freemasonry
Medicine **Biology** Music **Ancient Egypt** Evolution Carpentry Physics
Dance Geology **Mathematics** Fitness
Shakespeare **Folklore** Yoga Marketing
Confidence Immortality Biographies
Poetry **Psychology** Witchcraft
Electronics Chemistry History **Law**
Accounting **Philosophy** Anthropology
Alchemy Drama Quantum Mechanics
Atheism Sexual Health **Ancient History**
Entrepreneurship Languages Sport
Paleontology Needlework Islam
Metaphysics Investment Archaeology
Parenting Statistics Criminology
Motivational

THE
LOST TEN TRIBES.

By REV. JOSEPH WILD, D.D.

JOSEPH WILD, D.D.,
Pastor, Congregational Church, Toronto.

LOST TEN TRIBES.

BY

REV. WILD, D.D.

NEW EDITION

London

JOSEPH WILD, D.D.
Pastor Congregational Church, Toronto.

THE
LOST TEN TRIBES.

BY

REV. JOSEPH WILD, D.D.

OF TORONTO, CANADA.

NEW EDITION.

London:
ROBERT BANKS & SON, RACQUET COURT, FLEET STREET.

BY THE SAME AUTHOR.

Price 2s., post free 2s. 2d.
Uniform in style.

THE FUTURE OF ISRAEL AND JUDAH.

WITH A PORTRAIT OF DR. WILD.

PHILO-ISRAEL says:—"We recommend most strongly that all our friends should obtain the book. Once in their hands, we know they will read it to the end."

LONDON: ROBERT BANKS & SON, RACQUET COURT, FLEET STREET, E.C.

CONTENTS.

	PAGE
The Great Seal	2
Preface	11

DISCOURSE I.

KEY DISTINCTIONS 17

DISCOURSE II.

ISRAEL AND THE GATES.

ISRAEL—How the Gates of his enemies are to be given him—By this sign Lost Israel may be known—The giving will correspond to the multiplying—The promise, in this day, is rapidly fulfilling—England, Disraeli, "Tancred," and Russia 25

DISCOURSE III.

ISRAEL AND TERRITORY.

Promises to Israel—Material nature—Location of the Tribes in Christ's day—God's Providence—British and American rule—"Life from the dead"—Teaching the Nations peaceful arbitration—England and Russia—Afghanistan falls to Anglo-Israel—God's political geography — Anglo-Saxon evangelisation — Russia opposing it—British and Russian outposts in contact—Wail of Judah—Earth's girdle 36

DISCOURSE IV.

ISRAEL AND POPULATION.

Prophetic latter days—Our bearings in the ages—Unwise impatience—Israel to be always a nation—Her Empire—Historic career of and future of England, America, and Judah—Relative increase of population—The Infidel Saxon—Jewish, British, and American interests one—A full end of all nations but Israel—Famine henceforth only for the heathen—Arbitration to be enforced by Israel—American absorption—Startling figures of future population—The balance of power 46

DISCOURSE V.
ISRAEL AND LANGUAGE.
Latter day prophetic promises—Time of Israel's revival—Pyramid testimony—British Island population in 1882—Affinity between the English and Hebrew—Cell of the honey bee—Origin of language—Lion of languages—Foreign testimony—All tongues indigenous but English—The pre-millennial tokens 56

DISCOURSE VI.
ISRAEL AND GENTILE FULNESS.
Meaning of the Gentile fulness—Blessings through Judah and Ephraim—Best religion—Jews outwitted—Why Benjamin was kept at Jerusalem—French Protestantism—Gentile fulness contemporary with to-day—What is it?—Turkey exceptional .. 66

DISCOURSE VII.
DREAM IMAGE OF NEBUCHADNEZZAR.
Future history of the world—The destruction of the Papacy commenced—Ireland to be free and independent of England and Rome—Future glory of Britain and the United States 76

DISCOURSE VIII.
LITTLE HORN AND TURKEY.
The Turks the Ishmaelites—England and Russia to partition the Mahommedam Empire—Why England sympathises with Turkey 84

DISCOURSE IX.
LITTLE HORN AND ANTI-CHRIST.
Prophetic wonders—Twenty marks of the monster—The Berlin Congress—Anti-Christs many—Mistakes by writers 92

DISCOURSE X.

ANTI-CHRIST AND LITTLE HORN.

Second Discourse on the monster—Who he will be and his name—How he will obtain power—Trouble for Germany, France, and Russia—Communism—Romanism—Shakers — Matthias, Westchester prophet 100

DISCOURSE XI.

THE TWO WITNESSES.

Troublous times—Appearance of the witnesses—Who they are—How they can be identified—Their mission work and suffering—The time and circumstances of Christ's coming 109

DISCOURSE XII.

MOSES AND ELIJAH.

More about the two witnesses—Mormonism—God ruling among the nations—Career of the two witnesses—Anti-Christ—The throne and House of David 116

DISCOURSE XIII.

BATTLE OF ARMAGEDDON.

The combatants on both sides—Who "The Kings of the East" are—The great Napoleonic idea—Disraeli, Lincoln, and Grant—England's policy in Turkey—Future wars and intrigues—The great battle field—Gathering of the nations—Earthquakes—Jerusalem as a seaport 125

DISCOURSE XIV.

ARMAGEDDON AND THE PYRAMID.

The forces in the battle—Time of its occurrence—Mistakes of Adventists—A Church "strike" wanted — History of the world till 1935—Hine's theory 134

DISCOURSE XV.

WONDERS OF THE FUTURE.

Purpose of the flood—The Abrahamic current—Rending Mount Olivet—Former earthquakes—Boundaries of Palestine—Dan and Gad to guard the "gates"—Gad the Scotchman—The future Jerusalem—The Dead Sea and the Mediterranean to be joined—Mistake of spiritualising everything 143

CONTENTS.

DISCOURSE XVI.
NINETEEN HUNDRED AND FIFTY-SEVEN.
"Signs of the times"—The return to Jerusalem—Forces of Russia and England—Present locality of ancient nations—Origin of American Republicanism—Federation of the nations coming—Evolution and Devolution 149

DISCOURSE XVII.
THE STONE WITNESS.
The Great Pyramid—Who Job was—Who built the Pyramid—What it was built for—An epitome of the earth—The history of man contained in it, past and future—Science and the Bible, etc., etc. 159

DISCOURSE XVIII.
SIGNS AND WONDERS.
Egypt Past and Future—The stone prophet in the wilderness—No war for four years—Prussia ancient Assyria—England and Egypt to beallies—The future history of the world—The Philistines the Southern Irish—Who their great ancestor was, etc. 168

DISCOURSE XIX.
THE THRONE OF DAVID.
England's prophecy fulfilled in the Berlin Congress—The harp of Tara the harp of Israel—The future European alliances—Royal succession of the House of Israel 175

DISCOURSE XX.
JEREMIAH AND ST. PATRICK.
The prophet's commission—His life—The tribes in his day—Landing of Jeremiah in Ireland—What he brought with him—Colonisation of Ireland—Jeremiah the founder of the ancient Irish government and religion—Tea Tephi and Heremon—The ancient Irish flag—The harp and lion—Season of Ireland's historical prestige—Causes of her decline—St. Patrick a Benjaminite—How Rome destroyed Jeremiah's memory among the Irish—Destruction of Tara—Ulster never conquered—Irish independence—Ark of the covenant—Ruin of Tara 190

PREFACE.

THE following Discourses are presented to the public in book form, agreeable to the request of numerous friends. I have selected twenty from one hundred and thirty which I gave to my own congregation during a period of three years. I have tried to have them lean one against another, to the end that the argument might be continuous and somewhat complete. The reader will remember, however, that the vast subject of which they treat cannot be fairly and completely presented in such a volume as this. Also, it should be borne in mind that the language, style, and structure, are sermonic. Pulpit literature, in these things, is peculiar and distinctively characteristic.

When I first entered the ministry, I made up my mind that I would try and thoroughly understand the Scriptures. I soon found that a large portion was of a prophetic nature. I set to work according to the usual method, but to my sorrow I soon discovered that the method and rules in general use for Scripture exegesis, among what are called orthodox authors, were very defective and unsatisfactory. The fact was forced upon me that the true method, or key of interpretation, was not in use. I was always persuaded that the Bible was a unit, and that the principles contained in such a unit were beautifully related:

and because of such a faith, I wondered more and more as I grew older why we had not a better key of interpretation. Men spiritualised at random, without any kind of rule, except their own fancy. In this manner they expounded the material history of the Old Testament. <u>The whole arrangement was a Babel.</u>

I had faintly discerned that the Scriptures made a distinction between the House of Israel and the House of Judah, and that the prophecies belonging to one could not, in fairness, be applied to the other; and that some prophecies applied to both. It always seemed strange to me, that the people which God said He had chosen for Himself should not be known. The Jews were always known, but where was "Israel, His inheritance?" Again, I could see no point in the Lord swearing so positively about David's seed and throne lasting to the end of time. Taking them in a typical sense, they were about the poorest types that could have been selected, because of the shortness of their existence, according to the general mode of interpretation. Just at this point of my experience I came across a book entitled "<u>Our Israelitish Origin</u>," by the late <u>John Wilson</u>, the reading of which confirmed me in my convictions, and aided me to a better knowledge of the good Book of Providence.

After some twenty years of experience, I began to teach the principles of interpretation embodied in these discourses. Some three years ago I began to give a series of sermons on the Ten Lost Tribes. I soon found my own congregation, as well as the public, were interested and profited with the same, as was manifest from the large and constant attendance thereon. By personal interviews and letters, I have been gratified to learn that many have been savingly and truly converted to God through these Discourses. Especially has this been the case with those who were infidel in faith and action towards God and His Word. I have received hundreds of letters thanking me that the key of interpretation presented had made the Bible an interesting and easily understood book. The interest created gave rise to numerous requests for copies of my sermons. The notice by the public press now and again intensified the interest and increased the demand.

After I had been preaching on this subject for some time, I made, fortunately, the acquaintance of a name-sake of mine, Mr. Joseph Wild, of Bay Ridge, near Brooklyn. On this subject I found him remarkably well posted. He had lots of books, pamphlets, papers, and maps on the matter, any or all of which he gave me liberty to use. Through him my attention was called to the valuable writings of our English brethren on this point; Edward Hine, Rev. Mr. Glover, M.A., Rev. Mr. Grimaldi, M.A., Philo-Israel, and a host of others, whose writings have helped me much. Our English friends have now a vast store of this kind of literature; while, so far as I know, we have no home production. This is one reason I feel satisfied in sending forth this volume.

For years I have been greatly interested in Pyramidology, in the teachings of the Great Pyramid at Gizeh in Egypt. Twenty years ago I had confidence to lecture frequently on the subject, and a few years since it was in my mind to publish a small work on it. The necessity of such work was wisely and competently taken out of my hands, however, by the appearance of a book entitled, "The Stone Miracle," by Rev. Dr. Seiss, of Philadelphia. This is a book admirably suited to beginners on this line of study. And if one wants to go further and be specially informed on Pyramidology, why let them get "Our Inheritance in the Great Pyramid," a work by Professor Piazzi Smyth, Astronomer-Royal of Scotland. To this man God has given a fine mind and a large heart for a special place and work. But what pleases me above all, is that this Pyramid, being the *Lord's Pillar*, and *His Witness*, should so finely tally with the Scriptures and Providence ; that the teachings of this monument are in harmony with the principles of interpretation, as applied to the prophecies in these Discourses.

By a few small engravings I have sought to aid the mind of the reader through the eye. In the Royal Arms of England there is considerable of history ; the position of the lions, unicorn, crown, and indeed all connected with it is significantly expressive. In these things, the accidental groupings, so far as man was concerned, were as much under Divine supervision as the blundering of the Jews in the crucifying of Jesus. So, Divinely considered, they Divinely reveal. We know not the mind of our fathers in the matter of selecting and composing the items that make up the great seal, but we know the mind of Providence.

The plate of the ragged old stone, called Jacob's pillow, is not very distinct, but it is the best we could do. As it is, it will aid the reader in forming a better idea. The stone in shape is an oblong square, about 32 inches long, 13 broad, and 11 inches deep. At each end is an iron ring, much worn and rusted. It is a bluish steel-like colour, mixed with some veins of red. It has been in its present resting-place 583 years.

The main idea I wish to convey in this book, is that God is

conducting His Providence through His ancient chosen people, Israel, whom I believe are found in the Saxon race. And His throne on earth, through which flows the purposes of Providence, is David's throne, which I believe to be at present the English throne. Queen Victoria (and God bless her) I believe to be of David's seed. The United States fulfils the *rôle* of the Tribe of Manasseh. Therefore, to understand the prophecies, Providence, and the present movements of nations, as well as the future lot and destiny of each, we must read the Scriptures in this light. God has made the children of Israel and throne of David his executive, in time, on earth. They are his executive for civilisation, evangelisation, order, and conquest. Through them God will conquer the world to a universal peace. As Moses was to God, so is Israel. Moses being a divine executor, was to the people a god—so is Israel to all mankind. Spiritual Israel will come through literal Israel.

I have expressed myself freely, and shall cheerfully grant reviewers, critics, and readers, the same privilege. I send forth this book with a pure desire that it may do good. Amen, so mote it be.

JOSEPH WILD.

Brooklyn, May 1st, 1879.

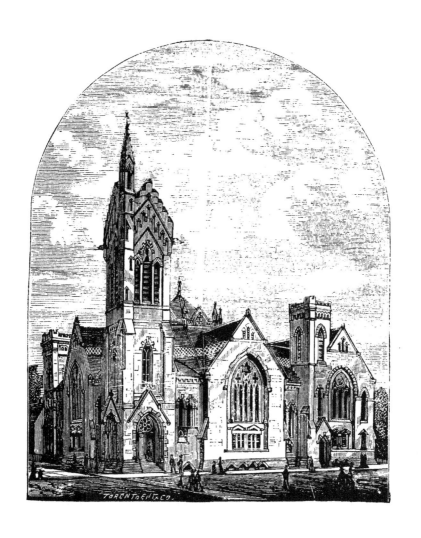

CONGREGATIONAL CHURCH, TORONTO
Pastor: Rev. Joseph Wild, D.D.

THE LOST TEN TRIBES.

KEY DISTINCTIONS.
Discourse I.

"We have a more sure word of prophecy; whereunto ye do well that ye take heed, as unto a light that shineth in a dark place, until the day dawn, and the day star arise in your hearts. Knowing this first, that no prophecy of the Scripture is of any private interpretation."—2 Peter. i. 19, 20.

I AM about to give you a few Discourses on Prophecy, and in doing so I desire, in the first place, to point out to you a few very important distinctions included in the prophecies. Suppose the Bible to be a great Palace, with its royalty, royal children, servants, and subjects. You desire to go through it and view it intelligently, and to understand all about its inhabitants and laws of government; now to do so, you must have keys and you must learn who is who, their place, authority, and work. If not so qualified, you could not pass from room to room, and you might confound the King with some servant, and visitors might be mistaken for the children of the household. Thus your ideas would be considerably mixed; you would be guilty of talking about the King when you really meant some servant, and of prophesying for the royal children in the name of the visitors. The years would come and go, but events would not happen as you had prophesied. Each generation would take your report and follow in your footsteps, thus confusion and disappointment would keep pace with the passing generations.

What is here made a matter of supposition, has been a solemn fact on the line of human experience. Men have studied the Bible and Providence in this ignorant and confused way. Theologians have thrown aside all restraints, and well-defined limitations and distinctions of the Bible in their assumed liberty of expounding and spiritualising the same. No matter to them that there is a God-revealed distinction between Judah and Israel, Manasseh and Ephraim, Samaritans and Gentiles, and the throne of David and the throne of the heathen. Writers and speakers are guilty of using the words Judah and Israel in a synonymous sense, though the words stand for different people, history, and prophecies, soon after the descendants of Jacob settled in Palestine. To aid you in seeing this historical confusion and folly, let me call your attention to them separately.

JUDAH.

What does this word stand for in the Bible? In the *first* place it is the name of the fourth son of Jacob. In the *second* place it was the name of his direct descendants, or Tribe. In the *third* place it became the name of the portion of the country occupied by this Tribe in the Promised Land. In the *fourth* place it became the name of a kingdom and government; this fourth name included the Tribe of Benjamin and their territory. In the *fifth* place it became the name of the whole country of Palestine, and is now often so used. To-day this word stands for those we call Jews, who, as they allow among themselves, represent and only include Judah and Levi.

On the death of Solomon the country and Tribes finally separated into two Houses, kingdoms, and governments. Nine Tribes went with Jeroboam, and three with Rehoboam—namely,

KEY DISTINCTIONS. 19

Judah, Levi, and Benjamin. The Nine-Tribed House was called Israel, the Three-Tribed House Judah. This separation was about 975 B.C. (1 Kings xii.). From that day to this these two Houses have never been united; but they are to be, as scores of statements to that effect are in the good Book (Hosea i. 11). About 580 B.C. the House of Judah was taken captive into Babylon, remaining 70 years, then they returned to their own land, and remained till the year of our Lord 70, when Jerusalem was destroyed and they were scattered.

Prophecies referring to the Jews are numerous, and in striking contrast to those that refer to Israel. 1. The Jews were to be a scattered people. 2. A specially persecuted people. 3. To be without a nationality. 4. To be without government. 5. Not to be owners of landed property, though they will have money, until toward the latter days. 6. They were to be a proverb. 7. They were to be few in number. 8. They are to retain a special type of features. 9. They were to be repeatedly robbed. 10. They were to reject Christ. 11. To retain the Mosaic service till returned to their own land. 12. They are to keep their name, and many such distinctions, none of which should be applied to Israel. All these things have been, and are fulfilled or fulfilling; and though men are wonderfully given to spiritualising, few, if any, venture to spiritualise Judah's curses. Men and ministers, calling themselves Gentiles, are rude enough to spiritualise the blessings of Judah, and, stealing them, apply them to themselves.

ISRAEL.

1. A name given to Jacob after wrestling with the Angel. 2. A term applied sometimes to all the descendants of Jacob. 3. In a spiritual sense, those who believe in Christ. 4. A name that covered and included the Nine Tribes which went with Jeroboam and formed the kingdom of Israel. They remained a distinct kingdom, and till now a nationality. From 975 to

725 B.C. they had some 19 kings. They were finally carried captive into Assyria by Shalmanezer (2 Kings xvii.). From that captivity they have never returned; as a body they never can, only representatives, as stated in Jer. iii. 14, "One of a city, and two of a family."

Now prophecy points out that it was Israel that was to be lost for a while, and come to light in the latter day. They are known in the Scriptures in contradistinction from others by such terms as the following: "*All Israel*," "*All the House of Israel wholly*," "*The House of Israel*," "*Men of Israel*," and God calls them His "*Servants, Witnesses, Chosen People, Inheritance*, and *Seed*." The lot, course, and providential portion of this people are very marked from any other, especially from the Jew, with whom they are so often confounded. The histories of the two peoples have been wide apart and as different as they well could be.

(1.) They were to be *lost*. (2.) They were to be *divorced* from the Mosaic law. (3.) They were to lose their *name*. (4.) They were to lose their *language*. (5.) They were to *possess* the isles of the sea, coasts of the earth, waste and desolate places, to inherit the portion of the Gentiles, their seed, land, and cities. (6.) They are to be great and successful *colonisers*. (7.) Before them other people are to *die out*. (8.) They are to be a *head* nation. (9.) To be a *company* of nations. (10.) To be *great* in war on land or sea. (11.) To be *lenders* of money. (12.) To have a *monarchy*. 13. To be *keepers* of the Sabbath. (14.) To have David's *throne* and seed ruling over them. (15.) They are to *possess* Palestine, and invite their brethren of Judah to return. And thus I might repeat some sixty positive marks and distinctions setting forth Israel; and yet men wilfully persist in confounding them with the Jews, or looking for this great and favoured people of the Lord among the lowest of human kind. Indians, Africans, and so on.

KEY DISTINCTIONS. 21

SAMARITANS.

The Samaritans were not Jews or Israelites, strictly speaking. They of course became Jewish in their customs and worship. Originally they were Assyrians. When the Nine Tribes were carried captive, they were brought and put in their place. "And the King of Assyria brought men from Babylon, and from Cuthah, and from Ava, and from Hamath, and from Sepharvaim, and placed them in the cities of Samaria, instead of the children of Israel" (2 Kings xvii. 24). The Jews and the Samaritans never wholly mixed; one was always distasteful to the other. They never were taken captive, and to this day they live in and about Mount Scychar, numbering between three and four hundreds.

BENJAMIN.

The Tribe of Benjamin has a singular and special place in the history of Israel and Judah. Neither the Old or New Testament can be well understood unless one understands the place of this Tribe in Providence. They were always counted one of the Ten Tribes, and reckoned with them in the prophetic visions. They were only loaned to Judah about 800 years. Read 1 Kings xi. They were to be a light for David in Jerusalem. God, foreseeing that the Jews would reject Christ, kept back this One Tribe to be in readiness to receive Him, and so they did. At the destruction of Jerusalem they escaped, and after centuries of wanderings turn up as the proud and haughty Normans. Finally they unite with the other Tribes under William the Conqueror. A proper insight into the work and mission of Benjamin will greatly aid one in interpreting the New Testament. He was set apart as a missionary Tribe, and at once set to work to spread the Gospel of Jesus. Most of the disciples were Benjaminites. Then, after 800 years of fellowship with Judah, they were cut loose and sent after their brethren of the House of Israel. It was needful that the Lion and the Unicorn should unite.

22   THE LOST TEN TRIBES.

MANASSEH AND EPHRAIM.

The history of these two representative characters is worth your careful study. The whole of the circumstances of Jacob blessing them must be accepted as Divinely directed. Manasseh was to be a great people, and so I believe he is. In the United States I find this promise literally fulfilled. This is the key to the settlement of this land; to the agitations of the Pilgrims and Puritans in England. The mission, work, and place of the United States may be found in the prophecies relating to this Tribe. Let anyone examine the great seal of the United States, and study its design, and surprise will fill the mind that facts, Providence, and prophecies do so wonderfully agree. Take the obverse side. Here you have an eagle with outstretched wings; the bird is perfect, not double-headed and deformed, as in other cases where the eagle has been, or is the national bird. The striped escutcheon on its breast, in its beak a scroll inscribed with the motto, "*E pluribus Unum*"—one out of many, as Manasseh was, and as the country is building up a grand nationality and oneness out of all nations nearly. Over the head of the eagle there is a *glory*—the parting of clouds by light; in the opening appear 13 stars, forming a constellation argent, on an azure field. In the dexter, or right talon, is an olive branch, a symbol of peace; in the sinister, or left talon, is a bundle of 13 arrows. But it is on the reverse side of the great seal that we have a wonder. Here we have an unfinished pyramid; a portion of the top is gone, exactly the same as the Great Pyramid in Egypt is at this day—anticipating this very day (Isa. xix. 19): " In that day shall there be an altar to the Lord. And it shall be for a sign and for a witness unto the Lord of hosts in the land of Egypt." Now it is somewhat singular that the Congress of 1782 should have adopted so remarkable a sign, one that would witness to God and tell of their origin. The reverse side is the under side, and shows from whence the nation came, and on what it is built. In the zenith—that is, above the top of the Pyramid—is a triangle surrounded by a glory; and in the centre is an all-seeing eye. Over the eye we have *Aunuit Cœptis*, which means, "*He prospers our beginning.*" On the base of the Pyramid we have in letters, 1776, and underneath the following motto—"*Novus ordo seclorum*," meaning a "New era in the ages." The suggestion of the items upon the great seal was from Sir John Prestwich, Bart., an Englishman. He gave the suggestions to the American Minister, John Adams, and thus the same were conveyed to Congress and adopted.

We have in the facts of the great seal a series of coincidents that connect this country with the Tribe of Manasseh. When the Tribes marched, Benjamin, Ephraim, and Manasseh went together on the West side of the Ark, for their homes were Westward. On their battalion banner was the figure of a youth, denoting activity, with the motto, "The cloud of Jehovah rest on them, even when they go forth out of the camp." Here we have the origin of the cloud on the seal. And when we remember that Manasseh was brought up at the foot of the Pyramid, and could see it from his palace home at Memphis, then we get a cue to the figure of the Pyramid on the seal.*

PYRAMID.

The Pyramid is a wonderful witness for God and His people. This building in Egypt has stood for 4,000 years; finished and complete, it stood for about 3,000 before anybody ventured to find a way into it. Then, at a great cost of men, money, and time, a way was forced in by an Arab chief. There surely is something remarkable that the only thing found in it should be a stone trough, and more singular to my mind, that the ark of the Covenant and this stone trough should be of equal capacity; and the laver in which the priest washed his feet in the temple

---

* Essay on "Manasseh and the United States," by the author, published by Robert Banks and Son, price 2d.

was exactly of the same size. And Solomon's molten sea contained just as much water as would fill the King's Chamber in which this trough was found. Can any man know these things and believe them to be accidental? Verily not. They do most assuredly pledge a God and Providence.

EPHRAIM.

This word is not only the name of Joseph's son and the Tribe, but it is used quite frequently in a generic sense, and stands for the Ten Tribes and Manasseh. To Reuben by birthright was the lead politically, but it was taken from him and given to Joseph, and so to Ephraim. From Judah came the Chief Ruler—that is, Christ; but the birthright was Joseph's (1 Chron. v. 1).

THRONE OF DAVID.

To this throne God pledged, under oath, a perpetuity. Also He pledged that some one of David's seed should always be on it. The throne and seed are pledged an unconditional existence. This being so, it follows that they must now be in existence, and that finally all thrones will be swallowed up by this one. Queen Victoria is of David, and the English throne is David's. Hence all the promises and prophecies referring to David's throne may be found on this line. For prophecy not being of private interpretation such facts may be proven.

GENTILES.

The word Gentile generally embraces all those nations and people outside of the Twelve Tribes. Keeping these few distinctions in mind, you will be enabled to read the Bible interestingly and with the proper understanding. Prophetic evidence is a strong kind of proof. Study the Word on this line, and you will find Providence and history lending glorious confirmation to the same.

ISRAEL AND THE GATES.

Discourse II.

Israel—How the Gates of His Enemies are to be Given Him— By this Sign Lost Israel may be Known—The Giving Will Correspond to the Multiplying—The Promise, in this Day, is rapidly fulfilling—England, Disraeli and " Tancred " and Russia.

" That in blessing I will bless thee; and in multiplying, I will multiply thy seed as the stars of heaven, and as the sand which is upon the sea-shore; and thy seed shall possess the gates of his enemies."—Gen. xxii. 17.

UNDER a divine oath was this prophetic promise made to Abraham. At the time it was given Abraham had, by command, offered his only son Isaac, which offering, to all human appearance, would leave the old patriarch again childless; but his faith staggered not, for human incompetence does not circumscribe the bounds of Divine sufficiency. The God who commanded Abraham to offer, recalled the command at a certain stage of the fulfilment, counting the faith of Abraham for righteousness. In Abraham's faith Isaac was really sacrificed; hence the divine approval: " By Myself have I sworn, saith the Lord; for because thou hast done this thing, and hast not withheld thy son, thine only son, that in blessing I will bless thee, and in multiplying I will multiply thy seed as the stars of the heaven, and as the sand which is upon the sea-shore; and thy seed shall possess the Gate of his enemies." An oath with men in this day does not mean much in the way of confirmation, but not so with God's oath. An oath ought to be sacred, and should be the end of doubt and strife. God made a promise to Abraham, and because He could swear by no greater, He sware by Himself. And Abraham lived to see the promise begin to fulfil, and to-day the heirs of Abraham may look and see the same promise fulfilling, for, as Paul says in Heb. vi. 17: "Wherein God, willing more abundantly to show unto the heirs of promise the immutability of His counsel, confirmed it by an oath."

Who are the heirs of promise? For to them belong many and precious promises, both spiritual and temporal. Spiritually, they are to lead and be responsible for the evangelisation of the world. Temporally, they are to be a numerous seed, a powerful people. They are to occupy the ends of the earth, the uttermost parts of the earth, the coasts of the earth, the waste and desolate places of the earth, the isles of the sea, the heathen, as an inheritance. They are to inherit the Gentiles, and make the desolate cities to be inhabited; they are to be the chief of nations; they are to be a company of nations; they are to be a great people; they are to possess the Gates of their enemies. Surely such a people should be found, for all these things make it impossible for them to be hid in a corner. One cannot help saying, with the psalmist, "Blessed is the nation whose God is the Lord; and the people whom He hath chosen for His own inheritance."

In the English Court of Chancery are vast sums of money, large fortunes waiting for heirs. The court frequently advertises for them, and many in every land respond and are eager to prove their claims; they are anxious to be known and accepted as the descendants and lawful heirs of certain testators. It is oftentimes difficult to establish their claims and prove satisfactorily their identity. The court demands that the evidences of heirship be very definite. In this they are right. But we venture to say that even the English Court of Chancery would not turn away a claimant who had all the distinct marks and abounding evidence of identity that mark and characterise the children of Abraham, especially so in the latter day, for then these characteristics are to be clearer and fuller.

The Jews are known; they have been known all down the centuries; they have not been able to hide themselves. In keeping with the Word of God they have fulfilled up to the present time the prophecies attaching to them. In all the world they are estimated to number some nine millions. The Jews include the children of Judah and Levi; these Two Tribes only. The Jews themselves consent to this statement, and allow that the descendants of Reuben, Simeon, Zebulun, Issachar, Dan, Gad, Asher, Naphtali, Joseph, and Benjamin, are lost, but not extinct. They are in the world, for God has not cast away His people for ever. If the Two Tribes give us nine millions, how many should we expect the Ten Tribes to furnish? Most certainly not less than forty-five millions. To the Ten Tribes the special promises of fruitfulness were given. To the Ten Tribes belong a greater portion of prophecy; and in the history of the world more is allotted to Israel than to Judah. Indeed, the world's history pivots on the Ten Lost Tribes.

I believe you know the God-revealed distinction between the words Israel and Judah. You know that they have a distinct history. Their place and work, promises and blessings, chastisements and rebukes, are as distinct and different as silver and gold.

The spiritual heirs of Abraham are all who are embraced in the saving and atoning covenant of grace in Christ. I do not say all who believe, for there will be more in heaven without faith than those with—namely, all those who have died before the years of responsibility, with many of the Pagan world who, never having heard of a Saviour, have therefore never denied Him. In a spiritual sense, they are children. I believe in this matter with Paul, who says, when writing to the Romans, chap. ii.: "There is no respect of persons with God; for as many as have sinned without law shall also perish without law, and as many as have sinned in the law shall be judged by the law. For when the Gentiles, which have not the law, do by nature the things contained in the law, these, having not the law, are a law unto themselves; which show the work of the law written in their hearts, their conscience also bearing witness, and their thoughts the meanwhile accusing, or else excusing one another." Thus, under the law which governs the Pagan, I presume many will be saved and many lost, just as under the law of the Gospel. In Abraham all nations were to be blessed, spiritually. In this sense Abraham's seed embraces persons of every age, clime, and race.

But who are the seed of Abraham according to the flesh? We answer, the descendants of the Twelve Tribes. Now to the natural seed the Bible assigns a distinct work and place. This natural seed is divided in the Bible, the word Israel standing generally for the Ten Tribes, and Judah for Two Tribes. These divisions have separate paths appointed them to walk in through the centuries. "All the House of Israel wholly," "the whole House of Israel," "all the House of Israel," have a special work. The Ten Tribes are especially called in the Scriptures the seed of Abraham. Sometimes "My chosen"; again, "Mine inheritance," and "My servant." God, in referring to them in their scattered state, and of His gathering them together, says (Isa. xli. 8): "But thou, Israel, art My servant, Jacob, whom I have chosen; the seed of Abraham My friend—thou whom I have taken from the ends of the earth, and called thee from the chief men thereof, and said unto thee, Thou art My servant; I have chosen thee and not cast thee away." The Ten Tribes are sometimes designated by the word Jacob. If we once get a clear idea who the seed are, then we can search among the people of the earth to find them, because in the latter day they were to be so different from other people, and distinctly marked, we will have no great difficulty in finding them. Of the special marks, one was they were to possess the Gates of their enemies. The multitudinous seed and other characteristics we will pass by for the present.

This seed were to possess the Gates of their enemies; of this we are assured by the oath of God. The word Gate here, you will admit, is used in a generic sense. It means a place of prominence, a position of strength, a strategetic point, as the entrance into a city. Remembering that in olden times the cities were walled around, the Gate was an important point of defence; or, as the narrow entrance into a bay, like the entrance into New York Bay or port, the Narrows we call them. Here the cities of New York and Brooklyn could best and first be defended. Again, a Gate in the general vernacular means any stronghold: a tower, an island, a mountain pass. Now, of this seed it is plainly stated that they shall possess the Gates of their enemies.

The text would be very finely illustrated if we supposed that Mexico held Governor's Island, in the middle of our bay, and defiantly dictated to us doctrines of trade, politics, and religion. As arrogant and as impudent as this would seem; yet such is the case with this seed of Abraham and other nations. Believing that the Saxon race are the Ten Lost Tribes, it then follows that the English nation is the chief representative of these Tribes, and that they should be in possession of the Gates of their enemies. Are they? We answer, Yes. And every year confirms and makes more clear the answer. This you say is a theory. Grant it. You know that in science a theory is formed and then applied. If you form a theory about the tides or formation of the planets, or this world, your theory with others is applied to known facts to see if it will fit them, to see if it will account for them, and to see if it is in harmony with the same. Now science accepts that theory which applies best, that which accounts for facts the most reasonably, and harmonises the most naturally. Such theory is then the science of the day, and will be so accepted and so taught until it is supplanted by a better. Try, then, the theory I have advanced by these rules.

Take the Islands of Jersey and Guernsey in the English Channel, between England and France, nearer to the French shore than England; the inhabitants, being a majority of them French, speaking French. Yet when France was England's greatest and most dangerous enemy, England held then, as now, the Gates of her enemies. Properly speaking, and adjudged by any human rule, they belong to France—as naturally as the island of Heligoland, at the mouth of the Elbe, belongs to Germany. Gibraltar, Malta, Cyprus, Suez Canal, Island of Perim in the Straits of Babelmandeb in the Red Sea, and Socotra, in the same sea; also Aden in the Red Sea, covering Arabia; Peshawur, the very entrance of or from India into Afghanistan. In and around the vast Empire of India you have Bombay, Calcutta, Madras, with many similar strongholds; Rangoon, on the Irawaddy river, commanding and even menacing Burmah. The vast empire of China is carefully guarded and held in check by such Gates as Singapore, Malacca, Penang, Hong Kong, and Cowloon. Sarawak in Borneo, and Labuan off the coasts, are such Gates. Africa is being gradually gobbled up; her strongholds and vast areas of country are falling into the hands of England; the coasts are fast coming under British rule. Recently England has come into possession of three Gates—namely, the island of Socotra, near the Red Sea, the island of Cyprus in the Mediterranean, and the Sublime Porte, finally the lofty Gateway, Constantinople. And it is now rumoured that England is negotiating with Portugal for Delogoa Bay in South-eastern Africa; price, three million dollars. But this people are not satisfied with all these Gates. They want—and they will get what they want in a very short time, thank Heaven; not what they deserve!—they want the famous Khyber Pass. This pass is a narrow road between mountain rocks that rise over two thousand feet at the lowest point. It is some twenty eight miles long, while for twenty-two miles the average width is only 150 feet. The Eastern end the English already hold, called the Peshawur Pass.

Afghanistan is a country in Asia. It is about the size of England, 460 miles from North to South, and 430 from East to West. On the North it is bounded by Turkestan, East by India, South by Beloochistan, and West by Persia. The population numbers about 7,000,000. They are as wild as the country is broken and irregular. They are chiefly agriculturalists. The country is rich in minerals and timber. In time past they have seldom been at peace, being very generally at war among themselves. Afghan is a Persian word, and means that which is wrapped around—no doubt having reference to the mountain chain that hems in the whole land. The people themselves, however, name their country Villayet, which means the land of our ancestors. They claim that in their country lived Adam and his children, also Noah and his. They say they had in their possession once the ark of the covenant, but they have lost it. While it was with them, if they took it into battle, victory was sure to be theirs. At the present time they have Noah's ark. It is imbedded in the ground, with a portion protruding out, which pilgrims to the top of Dera Israel Khan —that is, the sacred mountain of Israel—are permitted to see and touch. Many have supposed the Afghans to be the Ten Lost Tribes. It has been the folly of many of the learned, in time past, to hunt for, and actually expect to find, the chosen of God in some out-of-the-way place, to find them few, poor, and deluded—the poorer, the fewer, and the more wretched, the better. Hence, the wild Indians of the continent, the bushmen of Africa, the aborigines of Australia, the Laplanders of the North, and many such have been chosen of men—though not of God.

The Afghan country, no doubt, once had intercourse with Palestine. During Solomon's reign many Jews left the land as merchants. Solomon built store cities in Hamath, Tadmor in the wilderness, and many others. These store cities were on the great highway which he had made through the desert, so as to bring the trade of Dedan and Sheba to Jerusalem. That Hebrew names are given to the mountains, places, rivers, and persons, no one can deny; but such does not prove them to be the Lost Tribes—it shows away back Jewish influence and intercourse. They do not speak the Hebrew, but two languages called the Pukhtu and Pushtu. In either language there are few, if any, traces of the Hebrew. No doubt the Lost Tribes, after being scattered into Central Asia, when taken captive, about 725 B.C., wandered, some of them into Afghan, and probably for a time settled there, and gave names to the country. The Afghans themselves went into the country from India, and as the Tribes moved westward they left the Afghans in possession.

The Afghan country is one of great importance because it is on the highway of the march of Israelitish civilisation and progress. England wants it; and I predict she shall get it. Russia wants it, and at present seems to have the upper hand; but Russia, or England, or the world, can avail nothing against the purposes of Jehovah. The Gates are promised to Israel, therefore she will get them. Over forty years ago Disraeli wrote his novel called "Tancred." In this novel he makes the Queen of England the Empress of India, and one of her favourite officers is made Earl Beaconsfield; so far fancy became fact. But in that same novel the future of the East has been set forth. It was once very finely put by the London *Spectator* :—

"There is a story going about, founded, we believe, on good authority, that when some one quoted 'Tancred,' two or three months ago, in Lord Beaconsfield's presence, the Prime Minister remarked: 'Ah! I perceive you have been reading 'Tancred.' That is a work to which I refer more and more every year—not for amusement, but for instruction.' And if anyone will take the trouble just now to refresh his memory of 'Tancred,' he will see how much Lord Beaconsfield has borrowed from it in relation to his policy. Turn, for instance, to this passage : ' If I were an Arab in race as well as in religion,' said Tancred, ' I would not pass my life in schemes to govern mere mountain tribes.' 'I'll tell you,' said the Emir, springing from his divan, and flinging the robe of his nargileh to the other end of the tent, ' the game is in our own hands if we have energy. There is a combination which would entirely change the whole face of the world and bring back empire to the east. Though you are not the brother to the Queen of the English, you are, nevertheless, a great English prince, and the Queen will listen to what you say, especially if you talk to her as you talk to me, and say such fine things in such a beautiful voice. Nobody ever opened my mind like you. You will magnetise the Queen as you have magnetised me. Go back to England and arrange this. You see, gloss over it as you may, one thing is clear, it is finished with England. . . . . Let the Queen of the English collect a great fleet, let her stow away all her treasure, bullion, plate, and precious arms ; be accompanied by all her court and chief people, and transfer the seat of her empire from London to Delhi. There she will find an immense empire ready-made, a first-rate army, and a large revenue. In the meantime I will arrange with Mehemit Ali. He shall have Bagdad and Mesopotamia, and pour the Bedouin cavalry into Persia. I will take care of Syria and Asia Minor. The only way to manage the Afghans is by Persia. and the Arabs. We will acknowledge the Empress of India as our suzerain, and secure for her the Levantine coast. If she likes, she shall have Alexandria, as she now has Malta. It could be arranged. Your Queen is young. She has an *avenir*. Aberdeen and Sir Robert Peel will never give her this advice ; their habits are formed. They are too old, too *ruses*. But you see ! the greatest empire that ever existed ; besides which she gets rid of the embarrassment of her chambers ! and quite practicable ! For the only difficult part, the conquest of India, which baffled Alexander, is all done.' Who can avoid seeing what Lord Beaconsfield had been referring to in this passage—'not,' as he said, 'for amusement, but for instruction'? These were the ideas of his policy in germ—especially the treatment of the British Empire as having its centre of gravity in the far East—the use of the Indian army for conquest to be made in Western Asia—the acquisition of the Levantine coast for Great Britain— the active alliance between the British power and the Mahommedan power—and last, not least, the getting rid, to a great extent at least, by the help of Indian leverage, of 'the embarrassment of the chambers.' For a considerable time at least, English policy was evidently borrowed from 'Tancred.' The monarch, for anything we know, had been 'magnetised.' The Cabinet assuredly had. Lord Derby and Lord Carnarvon were treated much as the Emir in 'Tancred' would have treated ' Aberdeen and Sir Robert Peel ' —thrown them aside as two ' ruses.' "

England has indeed adopted an Oriental policy, and forward she must go to execute Jehovah's purpose. Russia is preparing on a gigantic scale. In Prussia the most flourishing branch of trade among the Germans at present is the manufacturing of arms for Russia. Though the late war be over, still Russia is buying ships, and fitting them out in America. She feels bitterly her defeat through English diplomacy; England taking Cyprus, assuming protection over Asiatic Turkey, and making Russia yield back to Turkey 30,700 geographical miles which was contained in the original Treaty of San Stefano. The following from the Government organ of Russia will give you some idea of her chagrin.

The St. Petersburgh *Golos* says that the Treaty of Berlin has produced an almost crushing impression on the Russian public. "It is felt that Russia has not attained her object; that she has been deceived by her friends, and that she has foolishly helped her enemies with her victories. . . . . What is the reason of our failure? One-half per cent. of our population have perished in the war, hundreds of millions have been expended, and yet the Eastern Question is not solved, and the Treaty of Berlin is merely a truce. The last war has clearly shown all our national peculiarities, as well as our moral and material strength. . . . . All the military requirements which depended on the inbred qualities of the Russian soldier were brilliantly carried out; but where knowledge and preparation were demanded we were not equal to the task. It was probably for this reason that we felt so much hurt on reading of the boldness of Lord Beaconsfield, who doubtless reckoned on the superior culture of Englishmen to that of Russians. All classes of Russian society are responsible for this. We do not estimate culture and knowledge at their true value. Most of us say that mental work does not bring money, and that culture is a means of corruption. . . . . In Western Europe, on the other hand, people have arrived by hard experience at the conviction that intelligence, capacity, culture, and energy, bring men to the front, and give them peace at home and power abroad. It is the knowledge of how to make the best possible use of their energy and abilities that has enabled the English to derive success from our victories and sacrifices. May this be a lesson to us."

But enough; one knows the end ere they begin, for the Word of God is true. We do not argue that the English are so much smarter than other people; no, but we account for their success because they are the executive nation of Divine Providence. It falls to the lot of those who do not believe this theory to account for their success without allowing them to be smarter.

ISRAEL AND TERRITORY.
DISCOURSE III.

Promises to Israel—Material Nature—Location of the Tribes in Christ's Day—God's Providence—British and American Rule—Life from the Dead—Teaching the Nations Peaceful Arbitration—England and Russia—Afghanistan and Anglo-Israel—God's Political Geography—Anglo-Saxon Evangelisation — Russia Opposing It — British and Russian Outposts in Contact—Wail of Judah —Earth's Girdle.

"Enlarge the place of thy tent, and let them stretch forth the curtains of thine habitations; spare not, lengthen thy cords, and strengthen thy stakes; for thou shalt break forth on the right hand and on the left; and thy seed shall inherit the Gentiles, and make the desolate cities to be inhabited."—Isa. liv. 2, 3.

IN the writings of the prophets the feminine gender is often used when speaking of the House of Israel, and the masculine when denoting the House of Judah. Quite frequently Israel is spoken of as a divorced woman, as being cast off, and as being barren. Judah remaining faithful to the throne of David and the temple service, and abiding in the land much longer than Israel, is presented as one married. So you will understand Jeremiah iii. 8, when he says: "And I saw, when for all the causes whereby backsliding Israel committed adultery, I had put her away, and given her a bill of divorce." Again, Isaiah l. 1: "Thus saith the Lord, where is the bill of your mother's divorcement whom I have put away?" Yet, though Israel was divorced, forsaken, cast off, and desolate, she was to have more children than married Judah. So the verse preceding the text says: "Sing, O barren, thou that didst not bear; break forth into singing, and cry aloud, thou that didst not travail with child; for more are the children of the desolate than the children of the married wife, saith the Lord." Then come the words of the text bidding her enlarge the place of her tent, or dwelling-place, to stretch forth her curtains, so as to cover over the new-gotten habitations. To spare not—that is, to be not tardy, or slow—in lengthening out her cords—that is, her influence—and strengthen her stakes—that is, her authority; but to break forth on every hand where there is an opening, and inherit the seed of the Gentiles, and make the languishing and poverty-stricken cities of the nations to be inhabited; in this conquest to go on and fear not.

These exhortations are given, and promises are made to Israel after she had left Palestine. No one can say truthfully that they have yet been fulfilled in no degree or sense, unless they find such fulfilment in the conquests of the Saxon race. These predictions cannot apply to the Jews, for they are few, nationless, and without a government. Touching the past history of both Judah and Israel in Palestine, we shall find it to be barren of victories, territory, acquisition, and number, in comparison to other nations. They have never occupied the land given to Abraham in fulness. In Solomon's time they bare rule only over a part of it. The Gentiles and heathens have occupied it more and longer than the Sons of Abraham. But what failed to be accomplished in the past, is held grandly in reserve for this day, the next few years. God will remember His promise to Abraham, Isaac, Jacob and David. He will remember it to fulfil it, in spite of hell or earth.

We have been blind and guilty in the past, unconscious of our origin, and, as a natural consequence, ignorant of our place and special work. In interpreting the Word of God we have been lavish in spiritualising, and greedy in materialising, overlooking the fact that nine-tenths of the Old Testament is a material history about one people, and that through them God's special providence was to flow to all other nations; and the New Testament plants the life and prosperity of the Gentile world upon the course and progress of Israel. God said to Abraham, "In thee shall all the families of the earth be blessed;" and more, "and in thy seed shall all the nations of the earth be blessed." Israel, being scattered and cast off, became a blessing to the world. They gave to the surrounding nations the only true idea of God, for in their lowest condition and idolatry they preserved the name and knowledge of Jehovah, and Christ sent His disciples after them through one of their own Tribe—namely, Benjamin—telling them not to go into the way of the Gentiles, nor into the cities of the Samaritans, "but go rather to the lost sheep of the House of Israel." To these sheep Christ declares He was sent. Where were these sheep? They were scattered about in Central Asia—in Scriptural language in Cappadocia, Galatia, Pampheylia, Lydia, Bithynia, and round about Illyricum. From these very regions came the Saxons: from here they spread abroad North and West, being the most Christian of any people on the face of the earth then, as well as now. Their reception of the Gospel gave them power over the surrounding nations, to whom they were, as it had been foretold, witnesses for Jesus and providence in a very special manner. What then, we say with Paul, will be the blessing of Israel—recognised and fully restored to God's favour? If so much good was carried and bestowed upon the Gentile nations because Israel was scattered, how much, and what are the blessings in store for those nations when Israel and Judah be restored? Paul compares it to a resurrection—like as when the barrenness and desolation of a Winter is supplanted by the fruits and beauties of Summer. "If the casting away of them be the reconciling of the world, what shall the receiving of them be but life from the dead?" (Rom. xi. 15).

It is reasonable to suppose that this world is subject to the providence of God. Such a supposition is grandly sustained by the laws and operations of nature without, and the experience and intuitions of the mind within; and I believe this providence to be all-comprehensive, bounding, and cognising all things, past, present, and future, both small and great; claiming the ages for its measure, the universe for the field of its operations, and the Infinite as the source of power. "The Lord Jehovah reigns, let the earth rejoice." Let me persuade you to thoroughly believe in the precision, the intimacy, and the completeness of this providence. This doctrine we need to fully learn and accept. " In the beginning God created the heavens and the earth," and it is He " who hath measured the waters in the hollow of His hand, and meted out heaven with a span, and comprehended the dust of the earth in a measure, and weighed the mountains in scales, and the hills in a balance." Aye, and more, yet closer still does this providence approach us in our affairs. " By Him kings reign and princes decree judgment. He bringeth the princes to nothing; He maketh the judges of the earth as vanity." Even closer yet, for without His permission a sparrow cannot fall to the ground; and so intimate is He with us, that He knoweth the number of the hairs of the head. Now all this kind of Bible instruction is intended to teach the nearness of God to us, and His interest and intimacy with nations and nature. Let us not think for a moment that nations can rush to war and be outside this circle of providence. Let us study to know God's mind, His plans and purposes with the nations; for rest satisfied that His plan will finally be accepted by men and nations, and His purposes will prevail. Kings may plan, diplomatists may diplomatise, scientists may analyse, theologians may teach and preach their isms, and politicians may make platforms and construct rings, yet none, nor all combined, can stay the hand of God. " He doeth according to His will in the armies of heaven and among the inhabitants of the earth." He can initiate, permit, modify, and destroy. Once we truly recognise the sovereignty of God over us, conceit will lie dead at the feet of humility.

The Church at large has but a slender hold upon this great

doctrine. They look upon the great movement of wars and strife, rising and falling of nations, as looks the country stranger upon a railway engine for the first time, the whirling wheels, the steam and smoke and burnished boiler rivet his attention so completely, that he sees not the driver in his car. So men are dazed with the show and pomp of courts and councils, with the harangues of legislators and march of regiments, that they discern not the master hand behind that directs all. "Verily, Thou art a God that hidest Thyself." No, no, friends; English bravery nor American ingenuity will not account for all that England has done on the line of victories, and the marvellous and rapid growth of these United States. As God said long ago through Moses, so He could say to-day—for heavenly counsel was given to the children of Israel on entering the Promised Land, with a design of suppressing their pride and enabling them to form a correct idea of their success in driving the strong and greater nations of Canaanites and Philistines—" Speak not thou in thine heart, after, that the Lord thy God hath cast them out from before thee saying: For my righteousness the Lord hath brought me into possess this land; but for the wickedness of these nations the Lord doth drive them out from before thee. Not for thy righteousness, or the uprightness of thine heart, dost thou go to possess the land, but for the wickedness of those nations the Lord thy God doth drive them out from before thee, that He may perform the word which the Lord sware unto thy fathers, Abraham, Isaac, and Jacob. Understand, therefore, that the Lord thy God giveth thee not this good land to possess it for thy righteousness, for thou art a stiff-necked people " (Deut. ix. 4).

By the same rule and for the very same reason that Israel conquered Palestine, does England go on from conquest to conquest. And because God remembered to perform His promises made to the patriarchs upon their seed, America was opened for the Puritans, who are without doubt the descendants and representatives of Manasseh, of whom God said " he should be a people, a great people."

The rule of England and America over other people, is to be as life from the dead—that is, whatsoever country England conquers and rules, it is better for the people, and the country, and the world. They give to the people a liberty that they would not have given to themselves; they develop the resources of the country as never before; and by trade and commerce bless the people and cause them to be a blessing unto others. And better still, they make known to the conquered ones, in due time, the riches of faith in Christ. So we have no hesitation in saying, a thing patent to every unprejudiced observer, that the aborigines of the conquered colonies of Great Britain are treated better by their conquerors than they ever treated themselves. The Africans, in the conquered colonies of Africa, are better off under British rule than those colonies or portions unconquered are. The hosts of India enjoy more, fare better in every grace and virtue in all that goes to adorn and develop mankind, under the British government and protection, than they ever did or would under self-government. So the French, Germans, Italians, Russians, Spaniards, and the numerous progeny of emigrants to this country, fare better in every way with Manasseh, than they did in their own lands. Of course, both in England's rule and America's there are many defects; but taking all in all, the good will out-weigh the bad; and more so as the years roll on.

True, an arbitrary purpose and an individualism is seen on the surface, yet under it all there is the hand of God. The farmer is free as to what he sows, but the Divine, without interfering with his freedom, regulates the harvest to plenty or famine. The Saxon people, England and America, stand in a new light to the world by the teachings of the Bible. Being Israel or the Ten Lost Tribes, they become at once the chosen agents of God for the glorious purpose of evangelising the whole world, and finally, by reducing the whole earth to the plane of universal liberty and peace.

It was necessary that these two nations should first be taught the art of mediation, for the ends of peace; that they should learn and show to the world that national disputes and grievances can be settled without an appeal to the sword. Hence we have, and what is much better, the world has, Geneva and Alabama and the fish bounty treaty of Canada and the United States. Not all the press did on either side, nor all the carping and blustering of individuals, could prevent the happy consummation of both these treaties. To God be praise, for they are prophetic harbingers of a better day coming.

No hand, nor power, nor combination of powers, can stop the onward march of Israel to her God-ordained goal. Her future is to spread on the right hand and on the left. Island after island, colony after colony, will fall into her hands for mutual benefit. Russia may contest this march, and will, for she is as much the appointed agent of contest from Heaven as England is to advance. In a few years she will try to take the place of England among the nations, as she has just done in Afghan. Russia promised, no doubt, that she would and could protect the Ameer against England, but the bargain was outside of the aims of Providence, hence it could not be sustained. It is ordained of Heaven that Afghan eventually fall into the hands of England—that is, Israel.

Against this fate-like division of the world Russia is going to contend and fight whenever she gets a chance. It would pay Russia and many other countries to read that " When the Most High divided to the nations their inheritance, when He separated the sons of Adam, He set the bounds of the people according to the children of Israel " (Deut. xxxii. 8). These bounds God will maintain wherever they run; whatever country they cut in two, no matter, the earth must finally conform to this Divine geography. This purpose is strongly set forth by Isaiah xliv. 7: "And who, as I, shall call and shall declare it, and set it in order for Me, since I appointed the ancient people? and the things that are coming and shall come." This same sturdy fact is taught by Paul when speaking to the Athenians, telling them that God "hath made of one blood all nations of men to dwell on the face of the earth, *and hath determined the time before appointed, and the bounds of their habitations.*" National destinies are not so much things of chance, or prizes for the sword, as many think. God promised to David, when both Israel and Judah were prosperously settled in Palestine under David's reign, that He would appoint a place for His people Israel, and plant them there, and they should not be moved, neither should the wicked afflict them, as aforetime (2 Sam. vii. 10). This promise God has kept. He has given them the British Isles, where none can afflict them, as they were wont to do when Israel was scattered in Asia and Europe. God has found Manasseh a home in this land of blessings and rich acres.

England, by a necessity, was forced to find new countries to provide for her multiplying population. Then she is forced to enter other nations as a missionary. She, with Manasseh, is chiefly responsible for the evangelisation of the world, and of course they are at work all over the world, for England and the United States send out more missionaries than all the world beside. Russia needs no land for colonisation, for now her inhabitants number only thirty-four to the square mile, while England numbers 389. If we take in all the territory under Russia and England, even then England has more to the square mile than Russia. Russia comprises about 8,000,000 square miles, and England, with her late additions, leaving out the United States, numbers nearly 10,000,000. Joining Ephraim and Manasseh together, they own one fourth of the whole world—namely, about 13,000,000 square miles; the whole earth numbers 51,340,800 square miles. Besides, Russia is not a missionary country. She neither sends any, nor accepts any, being at present the only nation closed to missionary operations and toleration. The past few years Russia has gained rapidly in territorial power. With the conquest of Bokara and portions of Turkestan, or independent Tartary, she has added some 800,000 square miles.

At the beginning of the last century the Russian advance forts were 2,500 miles distant from those of England. At the close of the century the distance was 2,000. Then in 1810 it was reduced to 1,000. And since 1855 it has been reduced to 400. And now, of course, they want it reduced to nothing by getting entire control of Afghan.

How wonderfully clear are the fulfilling events of the prophecy. This king of the North is to become a strong king, who, when Israel and Judah are settled in Palestine, will have spirit and power to attack them. So he is ripening, growing, and gathering power ready. Russia now comprises nine crowns, eight of which are crowns of conquest. Russia's one grand desire is to possess Palestine, especially Jerusalem. The Crimean war was waged for rights and extended privileges in this holy city. To-day Russian pilgrims swarm thither by the thousands every year. A few years ago she built outside the Jaffa gate what she called an hospice, which was designed to be nothing more or less than a fort. It is in a position commanding the whole city, and is a place of great strength. Often she has tried to possess the city and land. By-and-bye she will be permitted by Providence to pour her troops into this "land of unwalled villages," and when having nearly achieved the ambitious plan of ages, and nearly realised her one great national idea, she will perish to rise no more, "on the mountains of Israel." Her history is set forth by Ezekiel xxxviii. and xxxix. chapters.

Palestine and Jerusalem have borne undeniable evidence for prophecy and Providence. The whole land and the Book have been wonderfully agreed during the past eighteen centuries. How significant and telling the wailings and lamentations of the devout Jews, who crowd under the walls of the mosque of Omar, the site of the ancient temple. Here, each returning Sabbath, groups of Jews may be heard dolefully crying: "*Ali bene, Ali bene; bene bethka; bekarob, bimheira; bimheira; beyamenue, bekarob*," which, being interpreted, means, "Lord, build; Lord, build; build Thy house speedily, in haste, in haste; even in our day build Thy house speedily." Yes, mourning brethren of Judah, the time is coming when the house shall be built and the voice of wailing no more heard in the streets.

Can any student or inquirer after the truth fail to see that in our day a prophecy is being fulfilled? Can any one shut their eyes to the wonderful fact that Israel is breaking forth on the left and on the right? God has long ago said that Israel were the people of His inheritance, and that Jacob was the lot of His inheritance, or His girdle, or cord, as the word lot means. Then, if you turn your attention to Great Britain and her colonies, including Manasseh, you will see this girdle or measuring line around the earth. Let me aid you by pointing the same out for you. Look at the Eastern hemisphere circle, enclosing the Gentile nations. Begin with Great Britain; pass on to the Channel Islands; Gibraltar, Malta, Cyprus, West Coast African Colonies, St. Helena, Cape Colonies, Mauritius, Seychelles, Perim, Aden, Ceylon, India, Burmah, Straits Settlements, Labuan, Australian Colonies, Hong Kong, and the Dominion of Canada. In the Western hemisphere commence the circle with Canada and United States, Fiji Islands, New Zealand, Falkland Islands, British Guiana, British Honduras, West India Islands, and Newfoundland. Do we not plainly see that Israel is possessing "the isles of the sea," "coasts of the earth," "waste and desolate places"? These things are not hid in a corner; they proclaim the intentions of God, an over-ruling Providence; and who and where the Lost Tribes are. A miracle and prophecy are fulfilling before our eyes.

ISRAEL AND POPULATION.
Discourse IV.

Prophetic Latter Days—Our Bearings in the Ages—Unwise Impatience—Israel to be Always a Nation—Her Empire—Historic Career of and Future of England, America, and Judah—Relative Increase of Population—The Infidel Saxon—Jewish, British, and American Interests One—A Full End of All Nations but Israel—Famine Henceforth Only for the Heathen—Arbitration to be Enforced by Israel—American Absorption—Startling Figures of Future Population—The Balance of Power.

"Yet the number of the children of Israel shall be as the sand of the sea, which cannot be measured or numbered; and it shall come to pass, that in the place where it was said unto them, Ye are not My people, there it shall be said unto them, Ye are the sons of the living God."—Hosea i. 10.

A PERIOD of time is frequently referred to in the Scriptures as being the " latter days." It is, therefore, very important for the prophetic student, and the Church of Christ at large, that the time of days spoken of should be known. For connected with these days are a number of prophecies waiting fulfilment, and they are of such a nature that their fulfilment may easily be discerned. In breadth and scope they cover much territory and include many people. They cannot be hid in a corner, for the parts are so numerous and the interests so great. The fulfilment of these prophecies will make a radical and fundamental change in Church and State.

I take it for granted we are now entering into the time of the latter days—a time that precedes by a natural consequence the millennium. It is, therefore, unwise on the part of any person to claim that Christ may come any day, and that His millennial reign may be begun at any moment. It is but fair that we should carefully consider our bearings in the circle of

Providence and our position in the ages. The story and work of redemption are grand, full of interest and thrilling incidents; still we must take things in their order. Some stories we read are very fascinating. The plot culminates, the characters and incidents converge toward the centre in the hero. At such a point we are often carried away with our sympathy for the hero; we become anxious for him, and desire to know the issues, and so are tempted to skip a few pages and get at the end unwisely and unlawfully. Thus I think many are carried away by a loving desire for the millennium; they become anxious for the return of the Hero of redemption; they skip a few pages of Providence, and come to the end too soon.

These days are preparative, and in such a preparative stage we are warranted to look for the fulfilment of certain prophecies; for prophecies, indeed, of such a nature and character that no Bible student need be mistaken as to the time, place, and conditions of fulfilment. We have called your attention to one of these prophecies, and pointed out to you how the same was literally fulfilling before the eyes of all. God, in olden times, made promises to Abraham, the patriarchs, and their seed. These promises were nothing more nor less than prophecies. He attested the same by His own oath. He called to witness the sun, moon, stars, sea, night, day, the seasons, seedtime and harvest. These He called His ordinances. These ordinances may depart from before Him, but the seed of Israel should not cease to be a nation. They were not only to be a nation, but a company of nations. To this end, in the latter days, they were to come in possession of the ilses of the sea, the coasts of the earth, waste and desolate places; to inherit the seed of the Gentiles, and cause their desolate cities to be filled. They were to possess and rule over the heathen. In the latter days they were to possess Edom and Esau—that is, Turkey—and so come in possesion of their own land, Palestine. Now I call you to witness, and ask you if these things are so? Before your eyes, before mine, before the eyes of all the world, God is fulfilling His promises made to the fathers.

The very exceptions to the sweeping and comprehensive possessions of the seed of Jacob are pyramidal witnesses to the same. The House of Judah was to become homeless, without a nation and without a government, after they left Palestine; but to be a people known by the race feature, and by their unwavering adherence, attachment and fidelity to the Mosaic worship. This exception all can see, and none can truthfully deny. They have had money and men enough to buy and rule a nation, but as yet they have none. Their talent, their ability, and their money, have been the chief factor in the rule, prosperity, and greatness of many nations in the past as well as now. And the second conception is not less grand and conclusive. Let any one inquire what was to be the portion of the Tribe of Manasseh, and they will find that Manasseh was to be a distinct people, a great people; for so said the dying patriarch Jacob. Now such a people, a great people, we hold Manasseh to be at this day in the people of the United States. Some sixty colonies England has overrun, established, or conquered, and she is busy at work yet conquering and gathering in. But is it not remarkable that she has never lost one of the many, save the United States? Will anyone give an earthly reason for this marvellous exception? I presume no one can. There is, however, a Divine reason. Moses, when giving his prophetic benediction to the Tribes of Israel, gives us an insight into this question. Speaking of Joseph and the wonderful blessing in store for his sons Ephraim and Manasseh, he says: "His glory is like the firstling of his bullock, and his horns are like the horns of unicons; and with them he shall push the people together to the huds of the earth; *and they are the ten thousands of Ephraim and they are the thousands of Manasseh*" (Deut. xxxiii. 17). And further light is thrown on this

ISRAEL AND POPULATION.   49

subject when we notice what Isaiah says in the forty-ninth chapter. The children of Israel, when settled in some Isles, would lose a portion of themselves, and still the "children which thou shalt have *after thou hast lost the other*, shall say again in thine ears, The place is too strait for me, give place to me that I may dwell." The simple and natural interpretation of such a passage is, that the Isles referred to were the British Isles. The children lost refer to Manasseh, the Pilgrims and Puritans who came from England. And the cry for more room after they have left, shall lead England to look for lands in which to colonise her surplus population, all of which she has done and is doing.

Surely in these things there is something more than chance. Yes, there is a divine purpose fulfilled. Seeing, then, that God will put the land into Israel's hand, there will run another blessing parallel with this—namely a peculiar increase of the seed, or children of Israel, so that they may occupy and control these lands. These two prophecies are to be fulfilling on a parallel line at the same time. Are they so fulfilling? We answer, Yes; and the answer all the world may verify, for the facts are of such a nature that if they are not so fulfilling it can be very easily disproved.

The prophet tells us in the text that the children of Israel are to be numerous—to be numerous in an extraordinary degree—so much so that it shall appear partly miraculous when such increase in compared to other people, or judged by the common methods of reasoning. Hosea had three children; the first a son. He called him Jezreel. This son was set for a witness that God would cause to cease the House of Israel in Palestine—that Israel should cease to be a nation for a time. This idea Isaiah points out under the type of an abandoned wife. God styles Himself the Husband of Israel, and that He had given the wife a bill of divorcement. Thus the two prophets agree, and history ratifies both.

D

50   THE LOST TEN TRIBES.

Hosea's second child he calls Lo-Ruhamah. She was set for a witness that God would take away His mercy from the House of Israel for a time, and that God would utterly take them away out of the land. So He did; for a few years after this we find the children of Israel were carried captive into Assyria by Shalmaneser, and the Assyrians were brought and put in their place. And from these Assyrians, who were planted in the cities and country left by the children of Israel, we get the Samaritans, who were, as you see, not Jews nor Israelites by generation—they were manufactured Jews only. " And the Lord removed Israel out of His sight, as He had said by all His servants the prophets. So was Israel carried away out of their own land to Assyria unto this day" (2 Kings xvii. 23). During this captivity, which is even in force till now, barren Israel, the divorced one, was to have more children than the married one—namely, Judah.

We find that the third child born to Hosea is called Lo-Ammi, meaning, "Ye are not My people." This child prefigured the casting out of the Jews; that they would refuse to accept God in Christ, and He therefore would reject them. Thus the Jews became wanderers from their own land. And the land rests in desolation, enjoying her Sabbath of rest, while her sons and daughters are being chastised and trained for their return.

The time will come when God will call Israel to Him, and have mercy upon her, when the divorced one shall be restored to her Husband. "And it shall be at that day, saith the Lord, that thou shalt call Me Ishi, and shalt call Me no more Baali" (Hos. ii. 16). Now Ishi means husband, and Baali stands for Lord. Saxons have been looked upon as being infidels by the rest of the world. The Mohammedans and Buddhists never reckoned the Saxons as being the sons of God; and Catholic Europe and Greek Russia have looked upon England as infidel and heretical. And the Saxons themselves never went so far in their knowledge as to know who they were, their origin and work.

But the prophet says: "It shall come to pass that in the place where it was said unto them, Ye are not My people, there it shall be said unto them, Ye are the sons of the living God." And the time will come when Lo-Ruhamah shall become Ru-hamah, which means to have obtained mercy. And Lo-Ammi shall become Ammi, which means that this is My people. And Jezreel which was a sign of dispersion, shall be the sign of gathering. "Then shall the children of Judah and the children of Israel be gathered together, and appoint themselves one head, and they shall come up out of the land; *for great shall be the day of Jezreel.*" Then the Jews (Ammi) will call the Saxons their sister, long lost, but found at last. The Saxons (Ru-hamah) will call the Jews their brother, those whom in the past they have hated and persecuted; and thought themselves far removed from Jewish blood. Now they both will acknowledge a common generation and Abraham their father. And one with his eyes half open can see this part of the prophecy fulfilling. The Jews, England and United States, from this and henceforth, are one in interest, policy, and destiny.

These being the latter days, let us look for the signs of the multiplying of the seed so that they be as the sea sands God promised to Abraham, saying: "That in blessing I will bless thee, and in multiplying I will multiply thy seed as the stars of heaven and as the sand which is upon the sea shore; and thy seed shall possess the Gate of his enemies" (Gen. xxii. 17). Old Jacob foretold that Joseph would be a fruitful bough, whose branches would run over the wall—that is, colonise. This increase is to be seen in two ways. Let me direct your attention to one of these ways, in a special manner, because it is so singular and unique, so distinct and discernable. In Jeremiah xxx. 10, 11, we find a remarkable statement: ' Fear not, O Israel, for I am with thee, saith the Lord, to save thee. Though I make a full end of all nations whither I have scattered thee, yet will I not make a full end of thee, but I will correct thee in measure, and will not leave thee altogether unpunished." That Israel has been punished and corrected no one will deny who is acquainted with her history and sojourn from the time she was carried captive to this day. But has the other part of the saying been fulfilled? We answer, Yes—as the law of colonisation has progressed. The ancient Britons are no more; Saxon Israel has entirely supplanted them, just as Manasseh in the United States is supp'anting the aboriginies or Indians. They perish and disappear like snow before the rising sun. Not all we can do on the line of legislation, philanthropy, and religion, is sufficient to stay the ravages of this long-ago-declared decree of heaven. Go to Canada, and you find they are perishing; in Newfoundland they are entirely gone, and in every other province they are fast disappearing, save such as are saved by incorporation, by marriage, and salt stayed by the power of Christianity; but both these remedies are only temporal—they perish in spite of all in the heated atmosphere of Israel's civilization. Some few tribes may hold their own and seem to increase, but such does not invalidate the evidence of the decree. For they have perished in such numbers, and so uniformly, when in contact with Israel that history proclaims the decree fulfilled.

The native inhabitants of Van Dieman, called Tasmanians, have entirely become extinct. The Maories of New Zealand are rapidly diminishing. Fifty years ago they were 200,000 strong, now only about 50,000. In a few more years they will be gone. The same is true in all the other Australian provinces. The same is true of many isles of the sea, also of the African colonies. In these things, so exceptional, we can surely say with the magicians of old who contended against Moses, "This is the finger of God." Thus we see Israel increasing, by the law of diminution going on among the Gentiles. Israel in the latter day was to be blessed with plenty in the orchards, stall, and field, "For I will lay no more famine upon you, saith the Lord." In a recent year we learn that some 10,000,000 of Chinese perished in famine. India, in one part, has been greatly reduced in number by the same scourge. This country will be partly protected from the operation of this law—for no doubt a large portion are from Abraham. " But unto the sons of the concubines, which Abraham had, Abraham gave gifts, and sent them away from Isaac his son, while he yet lived, Eastward, unto the East country" (Gen. xxv. 6). This same scourge does not follow the colonising of other nations. It did not follow Spain, nor the Dutch, nor France.

If you turn to the prophets, you will soon learn how they are to increase in the latter days—not by a comparison on the line of diminution only, but in and from themselves. " Behold, the days come, saith the Lord, that I will sow the House of Israel and the House of Judah with the seed of man and beast " (Jer. xxxi. 27). Have these days come? We again say, Yes ; and these kind of prophecies are being fulfilled in this day in so special a manner as to make certain the times we live in. Through Israel, Judah, and Manasseh, the earth is to find the equilibrium of peace. The Jews will furnish the money, for in the increasing ascendancy, and multiplying power, and authority of England and America, the Jews will draw closer to them and invest more and more their money with them, because of greater security and profit. The balance of power and even compulsion will be in the hands of England and America, to force arbitration on disputing nations, and they will do so, having set the precedents themselves in the Alabama and fish treaties. At present, many will refuse this idea, and point to the famous Monroe doctrine. Now that doctrine has had its time; and it has served a good purpose for the country. The mercantile growth, and general producing power of this country, will cause us to abandon our selfish protection policy ; for of all other people on the face of the earth we will want free trade; for we will have the greatest surplus of mercantile and agricultural productions, and in a short time our very position and ability will push away all competitors. Once our mercantile and agricultural interests are cast in other nations, we will then have an interest in their wars and peace, and will be led to interfere.

The chief way in which the balance of power will fall into English and American hands is in the fulfilling of the blessings of the text: the multiplying of this people, first by natural increase, and second by incorporation and absorption. Look at this law of absorption; how vigorous and sure! If you turn into a field of grass fowls, pigs, horses, and cows, you get chicken-meat, pork, horseflesh and beef. The individualism in each creature absorbs and converts the same field of grass into themselves. So into this country are coming people of every nation and race, but the individualism of Manasseh will in due time make them all Manassehites. The children of the Russians, Poles, Spanish, and so on, become American in taste, manners, and sympathies. They are being grafted into the tree of Manasseh.

But look at the law of increase naturally. Take the population of several countries as given in the last census, and carefully note the relative increase, and how long it takes each nation to double its number. Russia, eighty-six millions, doubles every 100 years; Germany, forty-two millions, doubles every 100 years; Turkey, forty-seven millions, doubles every 550 years; Austria, thirty-seven millions, doubles every 100 years; France, thirty-six millions, doubles every 140 years; Great Britain, thirty-five millions, doubles every 55 years; United States, forty millions, doubles every twenty-five years; Italy, twenty-seven millions, doubles every 125 years; Egypt, seventeen millions, doubles every 150 years; Spain, sixteen millions, doubles every 112 years; English colonies, ten millions, doubles every 25 years. Now make a calculation for 100 years, from 1878 to 1978, and see how these countries stand in population and their relative position. Russia will have one hundred and seventy-two millions; Germany, eighty-four; Turkey, fifty-six(?); Austria, seventy-four; France, fifty-nine; Great Britain, one hundred and thirty-seven; Italy, forty-one; Egypt, twenty-nine; Spain, twenty-eight; United States, six hundred and forty; and the English colonies, one hundred and sixty—and that is not reckoning the natives in the colonies, only the descendants of the English. Of course, in a country like India, the natives will be a considerable number, and they might properly be reckoned in with the colonial items, and so swell the number of Israel's power.

Now these figures show a wonderful conclusion. In simple language, we find that in 1978, the English-speaking race, or Israelites, will number 937 millions, while all of Russia, Germany, Turkey, Austria, France, Italy, Egypt, and Spain, will only number 543 millions. Where, then, we ask, will be the balance of power? And why should this certain law come into operation at this time, if it be not the blessing foretold by the prophets? And can we not see that these are the latter days, and that God is fulfilling His promises to Israel?

The blood of Abraham and the faith of Abraham have been wonderfully preserved and projected down through the centuries with telling effect. And on this line the Darwinian theory of selection is very true, for the survival of the fittest is the proclaimed law of Heaven. There is power in land possession, and there is power in number, and if these two factors maintain their force for one hundred years, then we infer of certainty that the sceptre of rule and destiny of the world will be in the hands of Israel, unless the laws of nature are reversed, and the promises of God fail. The Word of God cannot fail, or return unto Him void; it must accomplish that whereunto He sent it and prosper in things designed; or as Jeremiah xxiii. 20 says: "The anger of the Lord shall not return until He has executed and till He has performed the thoughts of His heart; in the latter days ye shall consider it perfectly."

ISRAEL AND LANGUAGE.

DISCOURSE V.

Latter Day Prophetic Promises—Time of Israel's Revival—Pyramid Testimony—British Island Population in 1882—Affinity between English and Hebrew—Cell of the Honey-bee—Origin of Language—Lion of Languages—Foreign Testimony—All Tongues Indigenous but English—The Pre-Millennial Tokens.

" For then will I turn to the people a pure language, that they may all call upon the name of the Lord, to serve Him with one consent."—Zephaniah iii. 9.

IN the last two discourses we called your attention to two prophecies that are now fulfilling; they are on parallel lines of time and territory. The first had reference to the rapid accumulation of the lands of the earth by Israel. Accepting the Anglo-Saxons as being the children and descendants of Jacob, it naturally follows that the prophetic blessings and promises made to Abraham, Isaac, Jacob, and their heirs, should find a fulfilment in these, the latter days, and that such fulfilment should be found in the English nation, among the Jews, and in the United States. It is easy to see and believe that the curses prophetically pronounced on Judah and Israel have been fulfilled, especially on the House of Judah. The promises to the House of Israel are now being grandly realised. England is in possession of the isles of the sea, the coasts of the earth, the waste and desolate places, the heathen is her inheritance, and she is inheriting the seed of the Gentiles, and causing their desolate cities to be inhabited. From the taking of Jamaica, by General Penn, in 1655, to the peaceful cession of Cyprus, the course of this little island nation has been onward and upward. And if her conquests and progress are not amenable

ISRAEL AND LANGUAGE. 57

to prophecy for an interpretation, then the wonder is still greater. The facts are with us, and must be accounted for some way. The second had reference to the multitudinous seed of Israel in the latter days. Till two hundred years ago the Anglo-Saxons were not in this respect distinct from other races; indeed, for centuries they were distinct rather for their weakness in multiplying power and number. Many other races have exceeded them in this particular. But no sooner do we come abreast of the latter day time than we find the laws of centuries changed. In thermal science it is an axiom that heat expands all bodies, and of course that cold contracts them. But to this general rule there is one beautiful and benevolent exception ; it is in water; for if we start with water at thirty-two degrees, we find the remarkable phenomenon of cold expanding all below thirty-two, and heat expanding all above. If we take water at 212 degrees and withdraw it from the heat, it will continue to contract till we reach thirty-two ; then the law is reversed, and the water expands. Now the reversion of this law, at this particular point, is wonderfully expressive of Divine forethought and benevolence. By such a change ice is made to float in water, and so save our lakes, streams, and wells from being frozen solid. As this exception is to thermal science, so is the law of reproduction to Israel in this day. This people, who have been behind other races, now, at an appointed time, step to the front. The law seems to be reversed, and that, too, for a benevolent purpose —for the very purpose that they might be able to fulfil the mission assigned them in these last days, to occupy the new lands and evangelise the world. One prophecy seems to call for the other, for what would be the use of the lands without the people, or the people without the lands? It is an amazing fact that Queen Victoria should bear rule over one-third of the population of the whole earth, and that Israel, including Manasseh, should own one-fourth of the land.

But this amazing fact is made reasonable when we accept the Queen as being of the seed of David, and an heir to the promises attaching to David's throne, and when we accept the Anglo-Saxons as being the Ten Lost Tribes of Israel. Then prophecy, Providence, and facts, are a trinity—they are one sublime whole. God, speaking through Moses, said He would punish to reform Israel for seven times—and seven times, prophetically understood, means 2,520 years. If we allow that Israel were carried captive in the year 725 before Christ, then Israel would come into freedom, or be reformed, about 1795 ; because if we add 725 to 1,795, we get 2,520. Up to this point they were to be robbed of their children and to be few in number (see Lev. xxvi. 22). In the year 1795 Israel were to be relieved from these curses ; and about this time this special law of reproduction came into operation ; or, if we take the lamentations of Hos. vi. 1—3 : " Come and let us return unto the Lord, for He hath torn, and He will heal us ; He hath smitten, and He will bind us up; after two days will He revive us ; in the third day He will raise us up, and we shall live in His sight. Then shall we know if we follow on to know the Lord. His going forth is prepared as the morning, and He shall come unto us as the rain, as the latter and former rain unto the earth." By this passage, our day and the special providences of this period are mournfully and graphically referred to. Here a day stands for a thousand years, "for a day with the Lord is as a thousand years," so that when two thousand years should have passed by, Ephraim, who stands for Israel, was to be revived and blessed with fruitfulness sometime during the third day, or thousand years. In ancient time a day was counted when it had a majority—that is, when it had passed the half. The prophet here says we were to be revived, or raised up, on the third day. So, if you again take these three thousand-year days, you will find that two of them are to be completely passed, and during the third we were to be raised. The number we have given, 2,520, exactly meets the interpretation—2,000 complete, and 520 make a majority for the third day by the twenty over the half. These prophetic figures tally well with the existing state of things. About the beginning of this century England assumed to lead the world. It is a remarkable coincidence that, in the last century, the question of how to multiply the population was a subject of debate and legislation in the British Parliament. But what legislation failed to do, God in His providence did at the appointed time.

It is a curious fact, and well worth noticing, that the famous witness of the Lord of hosts in Egypt, the Great Pyramid, forecasts what the number of Israel and Judah would be in the year 1882. As Israel is symbolised in the Grand Gallery, it is found that the cubic contents of the same, in inches, is about 36,000,000 ; thus by some this is interpreted to mean that inches stand for individuals, and if so, then England proper will have this number in 1882.* Whether this is a true interpretation or not, we all know that these figures will be about right. The Queen's Chamber of the Pyramid symbolises the number and condition of the Jews.

From these two prophecies, so sublimely fulfilling, let me invite your attention to another that is now maturing. It, too, is parallel with the other two. We refer to the peculiar growth, power, and progress of the English language. After Israel went into captivity, they were to lose their language and take or form another. "For with stammering lips and another tongue will He speak to this people" (Isa. xxviii. 11.) We will all agree that the English language is not the Hebrew ; and if we are Israelites, then indeed God is speaking to us in another tongue, for few of us read His Word in Hebrew. It is read to the millions in the English ; hence the millions hear

---

* This was written in 1878, and the Census Return of the United Kingdom, for 1881, was 35,050,118.

God speak to them in another tongue than that of Hebrew. Between the English and Hebrew languages there is an intimate relation, especially back a few years, before the English had grown so much. The Hebrew was a very limited language; not numbering more than 7,000 words. The English is now said to number about 80,000. The most lavish writer does not use over 10,000; the common average is about 3,000. In the English we have not less than 1,000 Hebrew roots. This, comparing the languages a few years back, is a large per centage. In names of persons and places the Hebrew is very prominent in England.

I take it for a fact that language is of Divine origin. Men have written on the origin of language from every standpoint; the majority of them trying to account for its existence without allowing so noble a source. The first man, Adam, I believe, could talk as easily and naturally as he could see, and hear, and taste. Speech was a part of his endowment. There is nothing more wonderful in a man talking than a bird singing, save that speech is a higher order of utterance. Dumb nature performs marvels every day as mighty and wonderful as man's talking. The honey-bee builds its cells, ignorant of the fact that such construction is the solution of a problem which had troubled men for centuries to solve. At what point shall certain lines meet so as to give the most room with the least material and have the greatest strength in the building? This problem is said to have been worked out by a Mr. McLaughland, a noted Scotch mathematician, who arrived at his conclusion by laborious and careful fluxionary calculation. To his surprise, and to the surprise of the world, such lines and such a building were found in the common bee cell. Now I hold that the same Creator who gave to the bee the mathematical instinct could endow man with the instinct of speech. Even to animal instinct we find a certain variation and permitted latitude in what is called adaptive instinct. So in man we find this same instinct of adaptation in a higher sense. The instinct comes into play when we suppose a number of persons separated from others, each living in different quarters of the globe. In such a condition, though of the same language when first separated, they would not remain so long—that is, in the primitive state of society. Thus, among the tribes of Africa, at this day, languages are widening and varying from a once common centre. So Israel in captivity would lose the Hebrew gradually. The language of the people among whom they settled was the Sanskrit, from which a score of languages have come—the German, French, and Italian, Saxon and others. The Saxon of to-day, compared with the Saxon of 2,000 years ago, is very different; so much so that for us to learn and speak it would be equal to learning a new language. Thus the English language is a thing of growth. In the year 1362 the Saxon was made the court language of England. From that time onward its growth has been wonderful.

The prophetic outlines and Divine place of this language may be seen in the germal foundations, which give unto it such vigour, tenacity, and capabilities of expansion. All the features of this language go to show that it is destined to be the medium of a world's intercourse, and that it very suitably belongs to Israel, in whose hand will be the destiny of the world. It is the lion of languages. It will grow anywhere, and by reason of its tenacity when once it gets a foothold it abides. It is peculiarly suited to the humanities of every race, clime, and condition ; there is no limit to its expansive adaptability. It is in a special manner voracious in the destruction of other languages; wherever it goes, it sounds the death-knell of all the rest.

Soon as this language entered Britain, it began its work of destruction. Before it has disappeared the real British, the Cymric or Welsh, Erse or Irish, the Gaelic of Scotland, and the Manx of the Isle of Man. The British Keltic is entirely gone;

the rest are entirely local. Beside these it ousted from the island of Norse, the Norman-French, and several other tongues that tried to transplant themselves on English soil. It is at work in every part of the globe, planting itself and displacing others. A few years ago French was the language best suited for a traveller on the Continent. But this has changed. Now the English is by far superior. And why is it that the English is supplanting all others? To answer such a question in a scientific way one cannot do better than quote from the great and learned German philologist, Prof. Grimm, of Berlin. He says of it: "It has a thorough power of expression, such as no other language ever possessed. It may truly be called a world-language, for no other can compare with it in richness, reasonableness, and solidity of texture." But perhaps the most definite and distinct testimony given by a foreigner touching the future ubiquity of the Anglo-Saxon race and language, is that put forward by Provost Paradol, a learned Frenchman. He says "that neither Russia nor united Germany, supposing that they should attain the highest fortune, can pretend to impede that current of things, nor prevent that solution, relatively near at hand, of the long rivalry of European races for the ultimate colonisation and domination of the universe. The world will not be Russian, nor German, nor French, alas! nor Spanish." He concludes that it will be Anglo-Saxon.

A British poet has presented in poetry the special features of several of the European languages, which we give:—

> "Greek's a harp we love to hear;
> Latin is a trumpet clear;
> Spanish like an organ swells;
> Italian rings its bridal bells;
> France, with many a frolic mien,
> Tunes her sprightly violin;
> Loud the German rolls his drum
> When Russia's clashing cymbals come;
> But British sons may well rejoice,
> For English is the human voice."

There are eight languages in the bounds of Christian civilisation that may be accounted powerful, because they are the tongues of vigorous people; they are the English, Russian, German, French, Spanish, Italian, Portuguese, and Scandinavian. But of these all are indigenous, except the English, so that they die if transplanted. Look at this country and behold what a cemetery it is for languages. Once the French had strong hold and promised to abide here; but it is now nearly gone, even from the State of Louisiana and Canada, the last places of retreat.

If we take note of the population according to these several languages, we shall see the prophetic future of the English. It is spoken by about ninety millions, Russian seventy-five, German fifty-six, French forty, Spanish thirty-eight, Italian twenty-nine, Portuguese fourteen, and Scandinavian nine. Within the control of the governments of these languages we find England to have rule over 255,000,000 people, who do not as yet speak English, and we find that the other seven have only seventy-five millions outside themselves. Here is an important difference. If we look at them by territorial limits, leaving out Russia, we find the English language to own 13,382,686 square miles, Germany 449,684, French 571,578, Spanish 4,694,811, Italian 114,466, Portuguese 4,028,311, and Scandinavian 1,308,830. The aggregate number of square miles possessed by these six languages is 11,167,620, which altogether, you see, own 2,215,066 miles square less than the English. The balance itself is more than Germany, France, and Spain put together. The English language is divided only into two governments, but the other six are divided into twenty-six, all of which governments are bitter one towards the other; each trying to supplant one another, while England and the United States are at peace; and will ever remain so. In one hundred years from now the English language will be spoken by a thousand million people. Thus we need no stretch of fancy to see that what the prophet speaks of in the text will be accomplished in due time.

This language will soon be universal; by common consent it will become the language of the world. All the changes going on among nations forecast its ubiquity. China, by an imperial decree, has just added to her language 700 English words. Her sons by the thousand are with us, and by the thousand they are learning our mother tongue. The Japanese, till a few years ago, carried on their foreign correspondence through the Dutch, but now they have changed to the English. Besides, in the 50,000 schools in Japan English is being taught. If science has an answer for this strange phenomenon, so have we. Ours is, that it is the will of Heaven. Confusion of tongues came at Babel as a punishment. By this means Heaven scattered the unwilling descendants of Noah. When Noah came forth from the Ark God bade him multiply and replenish the earth—that is, fill it up. Babel, however, was built as a monument of centralisation, for the builders gave as a reason for building it, "Lest we be scattered abroad upon the face of the earth." By a confusion of tongues they were scattered. Since then we have had some 1,500 distinct languages, and some 3,500 colloquials, or say 5,000 different forms of speech. At the present time 600 of the primary are dead, so that there are about 900 languages now spoken on all the earth, with about 2,500 colloquials.

When these means have answered their end—namely, to make us occupy all parts of the earth—then they will die out. It then follows that as the world fills, languages must disappear. So they do. The English and German were the last languages to come into existence. No new ones are now being made. Alphabets are increasing, because missionaries are reducing spoken languages among the heathen into a written form. The Bible is translated into two hundred different tongues. This itself will only lead the millions back to English. All ship papers are now made out in English excepting the French, and no doubt they will soon have to follow in the wake.

The day of Pentecost foreshowed the universality of some language. Pentecost was a type, and the English is the antitype. The strangers from Phrygia, Pamphylia, Libya, Pontus, and Cappadocia, mingled with the Parthians, Medes, Elamites, Cretes, and Arabians. They all heard the Gospel in their own tongue. The different tongues make a wall of division, making them strangers one with another; but the Holy Ghost took away this wall, and they were all face to face, able to understand one another. The same power that here multiplied the gift of tongues—giving to some several—surely could give to Adam one. Away with a faith that cannot give God credit with being the Author of language.

No sooner do we see England in guardian possession of Syria than the idea enters into the scheme of reform of extending the English language. The Board of Directors of the Syrian Protestant College at Beyrout showed their appreciation of this new era of British influence, by a vote which was to the effect that on January 1, 1879, all instruction in the college should be through the English language. The Arabic only to be taught as any other dead language. This remarkable action shows that British influence in Syria is hereafter to be more than simply diplomatic; it is to be an all-pervading and controlling power, affecting every interest of Society. Truly another Pentecostal day is drawing nigh—a day when all the world shall hear the Gospel in the language of Israel. In all these things we see the lively tokens and pre-millennial agencies hastening on the day of the Lord.

ISRAEL AND GENTILE FULNESS.
DISCOURSE VI.

Meaning of Gentile Fulness—Blessings Through Judah and Ephraim—Best Religion—Jews Outwitted—Why Benjamin was Kept at Jerusalem—French Protestantism—Gentile Fulness Contemporary with To-day—What it is—Exceptional Turkey.

"Now, if the fall of them be the riches of the world, and the diminishing of them the riches of the Gentiles, how much more their fulness?"—Rom. ii. 12.

PAUL, the author of this epistle to the Romans, tells us that he was an Israelite of the seed of Abraham and of the Tribe of Benjamin. The fact so conveyed it is necessary that we keep in mind, if we would interpret aright this epistle. He introduces to our notice three parties: the Jews, who include at this time the Tribes of Judah and Levi; the Israelites, who embraced the Tribe of Benjamin and the other nine Tribes that had been in captivity for about eight hundred years—the whole together are generally known as the Ten Lost Tribes. In the third party we have the Gentile. This word Gentile usually denotes and includes the non-Jewish nations and people. The Hebrew word *goyim*, in early Bible history, was equivalent to our word nation. It finally began to denote any people who were not of the sacred seed of Abraham. The Greek word so rendered is *ethnos*, which means a multitude or nation. In the New Testament another word is sometimes used in a more limited sense—namely, *hellenes*, which is translated Greeks. Ignorance of these three parties, their place in Providence, and relation one to the other, has given rise to much needles controversy and division in the domain of theology. Men have argued for an election and a reprobation, laying great stress on the 9th, 10th, and 11th chapters of Romans, that is in no wise taught. The election Paul deals with is a literal one, having reference to a distinct people, whom God has elected for a special work in this world. This people God calls "His people," "His inheritance," "His chosen," "His witnesses," "His servants." "This people have I formed for Myself; they shall shew forth My praise" (Isa. xliii. 21). Hence exclaims the Psalmist, " Blessed is the nation whose God is the Lord; and the people whom He hath chosen for His own inheritance."

It will be evident to any careful Bible reader that God called Abraham from Ur, in Chaldea, from his own kindred, for a special design. Through Abraham's seed Jehovah designed that blessings, temporal and spiritual, should flow to all nations. He selected this seed for His own training, instruction, and culture, to the end that they might train, instruct, and evangelise the rest of mankind. Through Judah was to come spiritual blessings, because from Him was the Messiah; and through Ephraim, as representative of the Ten Tribes, was to come temporal blessings. And this in the past has been the order of providential procedure; it is the present order, and it is to be the future. Look and verify this statement and order by an examination of the nations of the earth at this time, by asking yourselves the question: What form of religion among the many on earth is best suited to develop man, to conserve his truest interest, and crown him with the greatest measure of peace, plenty, liberty, and security? Surely to this question there can be but one answer—it is the religion of our Lord Jesus Christ. And it is evident that Christ came of the Tribe of Judah. If we seek among the nations for the best form of civilization and the best government, we shall find the same to be in the bounds of Israel and Manasseh—England and America. Here we shall find individualism the best developed, and liberty the fullest grown. In this conclusion the intelligent of every other nation will concur. We assume no risk in making this statement. Thus, without doubt, the world at large is greatly indebted to the religion of Jesus, who was of Judah, and to the Anglo-Saxons, for the best and purest forms of political organisations or governments. The Anglo-Saxons being the Ten Lost Tribes, it therefore follows that God has carried out the design included in Abraham's call, and the promise made that in his seed should all the nations of the earth be blessed. To us it seems to have been a roundabout way. Had Israel been obedient to God in Palestine, and had Judah received Jesus as the true Messiah, the state of the nations most certainly would have been very different to what it is now. Still, through all, and for all, the purpose of Heaven has been carried forward.

In studying Providence it is always well to remember that God is not dependent on the harmonious co-operation of His creatures for the accomplishment of His purpose. He can gain His ends either through our hate or love, resistance or co-operation. When the Jews had crucified Christ, they naturally thought they had cut short His career and cut off His influence; for so it would appear by all human reasoning. Even the disciples did not see how He could be the Messiah and Deliverer of Israel when He allowed Himself to be crucified. The hope of Israel was buried with the dead Christ. They had hoped that it had been He who should have redeemed Israel; but this hope was then dead. But by His resurrection they saw through the secret of Providence, and they saw that God was faithful in devising a way of escape, and able to bring to pass His own glorious purpose. So Peter voices their experience when he says, "Blessed be the God and Father of our Lord Jesus Christ, which, according to His abundant mercy, hath begotten us again unto a lively hope by the resurrection of Jesus Christ from the dead." The Jews soon found out they had made a mistake in crucifying Jesus; for the risen Christ was mightier than the teaching Jesus. They had crushed a seed to the earth which sprang forth in renewed beauty and grace; whose death was life and whose loss was gain. In common parlance they had been outwitted. They slew a man and He rose a God. They in wrath offered a sacrifice once and for all, even for the very sin in which they were then indulging. They unknowingly abolished death, and brought life and immortality to light. The critical and unbelieving Sadducees, who denied another life than this, gave aid in proving another and a better; for Christ risen condemned their unbelief. The proud and ritualistic Pharisee, who loved the temple and its gorgeous ceremony, destroyed one and made the other of none avail, for in the planted death of Jesus they laid the foundation of another and grander temple—one composed of living stones—and made the temple service meaningless; for the anti-type had swallowed up the type; the real, the ideal. In all this they had reasoned on a human plan, which is not high enough to wholly overlook and explore the kingdom of God. Paul, in 1 Cor. ii. 7, makes this matter plain: "But we speak the wisdom of God in a mystery; even the hidden wisdom which God ordained before the world unto our glory, which none of the princes of this world knew; for had they known it, they would not have crucified the Lord of glory." Jesus committed His life to the wave-tide of their rage, and was floated to death and victory. On the man side there was purpose and hate, and for this they were responsible; and on the Divine side we have wisdom and love working out the salvation of a lost race.

Jesus came to His own and they did not receive Him. Who were His own? We answer the Jews; for He was of Judah. But if His own did not receive Him, we ask, who did? The answer is, that Israel received Him. The Israelites in the land at that time were the Tribe of Benjamin. They had been providentially selected for this work nearly a thousand years before. This one Tribe of Benjamin has a very peculiar history? and if you will study it over, it will greatly serve to confirm your faith in the divine inspiration of the Bible and the unity and forethought of providence. The original theocracy of Israel consisted of Twelve Tribes. This theocracy was divided under Rehoboam, Solomon's son and successor. Ten Tribes seceded, and formed a kingdom, which is ever after called the kingdom of Israel; their first king was Jeroboam. But it is very singular to notice, that one of these Ten Tribes is lent to the kingdom of Judah, and this one Tribe is Benjamin. In this was the Divine provision for the time of Christ. We find in the first book of Kings, eleventh chapter, that Solomon displeased the Lord by his wicked ways, and the Lord said: "Forasmuch as this is done of thee, and thou hast not kept My covenant and My statutes which I have commanded thee, I will surely rend the kingdom from thee, and I will give it to thy servant (Jeroboam was Solomon's servant at that time); notwithstanding in thy days I will not do it, for David thy father's sake; but I will rend it out of the hands of thy son. Howbeit I will not rend away all the kingdom, but will give one Tribe to thy son, for David My servant's sake, and for Jerusalem's sake, which I have chosen." All the kingdom evidently meant the Ten Tribes. The same truth Ahijah, the Shilonite, taught when he rent his new garment into twelve pieces, and gave to Jeroboam ten. "And he said to Jeroboam, Take the ten pieces; for thue saith the Dord the God of Israel: Behold, I will rend the kingdom out of the hands of Solomon and will give Ten Tribes to thee." Then comes in the reserve clause again: "But he shall have one Tribe for My servant David's sake, and for Jerusalem's sake, the city which I have chosen out of all the Tribes of Israel." And the reason for the reservation of this Tribe is clearly expressed in verse 36: "And unto his son will I give one Tribe, that David My servant may always have a light before Me in Jerusalem." Now it is plain why this Tribe was an exception. The city of Jerusalem, God says, He has chosen out of all the cities of Israel, because to this city would the Messiah come. And beautifully agreeing with the forethought is the fact that when the Tribes had their lots assigned them in Palestine, the city of Jerusalem fell in the portion of Benjamin.

The Tribe then were owners of the city, and they received Christ. The disciples and first followers and converts were chiefly from this Tribe of Benjamin. After this Tribe received Christ, then their work was done in Jerusalem. So they were to separate from the kingdom of Judah, and seek out their own brethren and unite with them. The time of their separation had been foretold by the prophet, and pointed out by the Saviour. The time of their departure would be coincident with the siege and destruction of their beloved city. So cried Jeremiah down through the centuries, "Oh, ye children of Benjamin, gather yourselves to flee out of the midst of Jerusalem, and blow the trumpet in Tekoa, and set up a sign of fire in Beth-haccerem, for evil appeareth out of the North and great destruction" (Jer. vi. 1). If any of you are mindful to examine history; you will find that war came, that the destruction was terrible, and more, you will find that the Benjamites escaped. These points profane historians thoroughly confirm. Having fulfilled their God-appointed mission with the kingdom of Judah and in Jerusalem, Heaven gave them to be light-bearers to the whole world; first to specially find their own brethren of the House of Israel, and carry them the Gospel, and they would carry it unto all the earth. Thus the Saviour said, "Go not in the way of the Gentiles, and into any city of the Samaritans enter ye not. But go rather to the lost sheep of the House of Israel." Peter in his epistle tells where these lost sheep were scattered. Agreeable to the Saviour's command they went forth, and preached as they went, and so carried the Gospel of Jesus with them. As a Tribe they finally settled in Normandy, and gave to France her Protestantism, which, from that day to this, Catholicism has not been able entirely to uproot, though it has made several desperate attempts. They finally, however, as a Tribe, under the Norman conquest, entered England and united with the other nine Tribes. Their advent, and the way they came, is very graphically symbolised in the unicorn on the royal arms of England. The unicorn is looking Westward, and is attached to the crown by a chain—showing that it came from the East.

With these facts in one's mind, read those difficult passages in Romans, and all will be plain. Take, for instance, Romans xi. 17 : " And if some of the branches be broken off, and thou, being a wild olive tree, were grafted in among them, and with them partakest of the root and fatness of the olive tree." Here it is manifest that we have three parties mentioned. The branches broken off mean Judah and Levi, the wild olive stands for the Gentiles, the people in among whom they were grafted, or root of whose fatness they were partakers, mean the Israelites. The hope of Jewish restoration is nicely set forth in verse 24 : " For if thou wert cut out of the olive tree, which is wild by nature, and wert grafted contrary to nature into a good olive tree, how much more shall these, which be the natural branches, be grafted into their own olive tree." Again, the wild olive stands for the Gentiles, the good olive tree for Israel, the branches broken off, but which may be grafted in again, for the Jews. Thus to this theory of interpretation the whole Bible responds easily and reasonably. With this kind of interpretation one need not twist and distort the sacred Word in order to understand it. I trust the day is near when men will expound the sacred Scriptures by the rules of common sense.

The calamity that happened to the nine Tribes of Israel in being carried captive has been turned into good by our heavenly Father—into good for them and all the world. " Therefore the Lord removed Israel out of His sight, as He had said by all His servants the prophets. So was Israel carried away out of their own land to Assyria unto this day " (2 Kings xvii. 23).

Keeping back the Tribe of Benjamin is a marvel of goodness. And with Paul we may exclaim: "Now if the fall of them be the riches of the world, and the diminishing of them the riches of the Gentiles, how much more their fulness." If Israel had been able to contribute so much of Christianity to the world, and evolve in her imperfect state such an equitable form of government, what will her contribution be when gathered, restored, and once again put into theocratic relation to God? "For if the casting away of them be the reconciling of the world, what shall the receiving of them be, but life from the dead?" This people who have been scattered among the Gentiles God is collecting out from among them for His own glorious purpose and work. Thus scattered they have been a mystery—a mystery among the Gentiles. Paul to the Colossians says: "To whom God would make known what is the riches of the glory of this mystery among the Gentiles, which is Christ in you the hope of glory."

When will the fulness of the text take place? We answer, Before long. The fulness here stands over against the Gentile fulness. In the three last discourses we called your attention to Israel's maturing fulness in land, people, and language. And now, if you will consider the state of the Gentile nations, it will be apparent to you that the time of Gentile fulness is now present. These Gentile nations are now overflowing. Take China with her teeming millions, and ask why she has not peopled the world? for surely she could have done so long ago. But she barred her own doors by making it unlawful for any of her subjects to leave the flowery kingdom—forbidding heaven to such as should die outside. Now, however, she must permit emigration or perish by famine. Take the countries of Europe, and is it not strange that Israel's fulness of land, people, and language is made the fuller by these nations contributing towards the same? The fulness of the Gentiles is made to flow into the fulness of Israel. These countries, outside of Israel-

England, have no colonies to send their overflow to; hence, they are filling up the domain of Israel, and so hastening on her fulness. The French, Germans, Italians, and Spaniards forsake their land and language, thus adding to Israel's fulness; for they chiefly settle down within the bounds of Israel. To this Gentile fulness there was to be one strange exception—that was in the Turkish nation. This nation is set forth by the prophet under the figure of the River Euphrates. In their first appearance they were to be very numerous. In the eleventh century they began to invade Europe. The historian Gibbon, speaking of them, says: "Myriads of Turkish horsemen overspread the whole Greek empire, until at last Constantinople fell into their hands." From 1453 till now have they held this grand capital. John, in Rev. ix., pictures this invasion, and speaks of the number of horsemen. He speaks of them as having power in their mouths and tails. This language is very expressive when we remember the Moslem's war-cry, which was "The sword of Mahomet and of God." And in one of the first of their great battles they lost their standard; but, not long baffled, the commander-in-chief cut off the tail of his beautiful steed, and, putting it on the end of a pole, hoisted it as a standard. This ensign they long used. This kingdom, however, is to dry up—that is, to disappear gradually, as a river dries up. All this is taking place. Turkey sends emigrants nowhere. They are literally dying out. In number they are fewer each year. Turkey will pass away for want of Turks. Her territory will be taken away from her gradually. How remarkable the dealings of Providence with men and nations!

Up to the point of Gentile fulness, Israel was to be partly blind, for God's plans, through Israel, were to remain a mystery for a time. "For I would not, brethren, that ye should be ignorant of this mystery, lest ye should be wise in your own conceits; that blindness in part is happened to Israel, until the fulness of the Gentiles be come in. Our idea is that the Gentile fulness is now in, and if so, it is natural, then that Israel should be found, and about this time have her eyes opened. Up to this time of fulness, Jerusalem was to be trodden down. "And they shall fall by the edge of the sword, and be led away captive into all nations; and Jerusalem shall be trodden down of the Gentiles, until the times of the Gentiles be fulfilled" (Luke xxi. 23). Now, the Jews did fall by the edge of the sword, as the Saviour foretold; they were carried captive into all nations; Jerusalem has been trodden under foot. Thus, then, do we see three parts of His prophecy literally fulfilled; and so surely will the fourth part be, which is, that in connection with Gentile fulness this treading shall cease, and proud, imperial Salem shall lift her head once more free from tyrant hands and heathen tramping, to become the city of God and His chosen ones.

When Moses was sent to deliver the children of Israel from Egypt, he was equipped with miraculous power that he might convince Pharaoh and the Egyptians what was the will of Jehovah; but not more so than are the prophetic students of this day; for the presence of the Divine gleams forth all around in the miracles of prophecy now so wonderfully fulfilling in this our day.

DREAM IMAGE OF NEBUCHADNEZZAR.
Discourse VII.

Future History of the World—The Destruction of the Papacy Commenced—Ireland to be Free and Independent of England and Rome—Future Glory of Britain and the United States.

"Thou, O King, sawest and beheld a great image. This great image whose brightness was excellent, stood before thee; and the form thereof was terrible."—Dan. ii. 31.

ABOUT 2,500 years ago the kingdom of Babylon was strong, great, and prosperous. The king of this vast empire is known in history as Nebuchadnezzar. His reign had been marked with great victories over the surrounding nations. The mighty Empire of Assyria he had conquered; Egypt he had wasted and almost destroyed; Palestine he had reduced to strange and pitiable desolation, having carried the Jewish inhabitants captive into the region of Babylon. Among these captives we find Daniel, the prophet of Judah. In the second year of Nebuchadnezzar's consolidated reign, as King over Babylon and Assyria, he dreamed a dream which gave him much anxiety of mind and troubled him very much. This dream he could not remember nor explain, save that it had left a terrible impression on his mind. The wise men were confounded, for they could neither declare the vision or its meaning. The king, in his rage decreed them all to death. At this point appears Daniel, one of the captives of Judah. Moved of God, he presents himself before the king, and makes known to him the vision and interpretation.

The king had seen a great metallic image, excellent in brightness and terrible in form. It was a human figure of massive proportions, standing erect with outstretched arms, and of a mixed and strange composition. The head was of fine gold. The breast and arms were of silver. The belly and thighs of brass. The legs of iron, the feet part of iron and part of clay. While the king was gazing on this monstrous figure with intense interest, his attention was arrested by the appearance of a small stone—this stone was alone; there appeared no hands handling it or moving it. It was cut out of the mountain without hands. In this stone there appears to be a good deal of the supernatural. At once this little stone assaults the image, beginning at the feet. The battle is surely unequal; the battle continues, and during the struggle the stone actually grows; the image falls to pieces—the feet, thigh, breast, and head—and victory is with the stone. By the time the image is wholly destroyed the stone has become a mountain; or, as Daniel said to Nebuchadnezzar, "Thou sawest till that a stone was cut out without hands, which smote the image upon his feet that were of iron and clay, and brake them to pieces. Then was the iron, the clay, the brass, the silver, and the gold broken to pieces together, and became like the chaff of the Summer threshing-floors; and the wind carried them away, that no place was found for them; and the stone that smote the image became a great mountain and filled the whole earth."

In this vision and interpretation we have a line of history laid bare so clearly that we need not err. The beginning is the time and kingdom of Nebuchadnezzar. The image stands for four great earthly monarchies, extending down through the centuries even to this time and day—and a little further; for these monarchies are not yet wholly destroyed, and the stone kingdom does not yet fill the world. Of this fifth, or stone kingdom, there is to be no end by conquest, or decay, or succession. Daniel says that this kingdom shall not be left to other people—that is, it shall never be succeeded.

The peculiar features of the stone kingdom make it interesting to ascertain what kingdom, monarchy, and people stand for it; for such kingdom, though small at the beginning, is to grow, prosper, and continue to the end of time. Guided by the Scriptures and history, let us look for these four earthly monarchies; and the better to accomplish our task, let us stretch the giant figure on his back; then his head of gold will rest in Babylon, his silver breast and arms will take in Media and Persia, his belly and thighs will take in Greece, and his legs and feet will take in Rome. Thus, then, the gold head stood for Babylon, and is now in this day represented and found in Russia—for Russia is a continuation of Babylon. The *Czar* is on the line of Nebuchadnezzar. This gold-headed kingdom will be the last destroyed—the destruction begins at the feet. Russia, therefore, has yet a lease of life and prosperity; but, finally, she too will yield the contests and disappear before the stone kingdom. The gold stands for work and endurance, as the head is significant of supremacy; but the stone will finally destroy it.

The silver, next in value and endurance, of which were the arms and breast, stands for Persia. Centuries ago Persia was the great Power of the earth. At one time it would seem as if she never would decay or ever have a rival; but her day came, and she has dwindled down to the little kingdom and monarchy —the Persia of to-day. Her power is gone, she is consumptive, and will soon disappear as a separate kingdom. The late visit of the King of Persia to the Czar at St. Petersburg is not without meaning. The gold head of Russia will need the assistance of the arms of Persia by-and-bye.

The brass parts stand well and appropriately for ancient Greece—an Empire once so gigantic and powerful, a people so polished and learned, but long ago their time, and work, and place were marked out. And now the time is nearly gone and the work done, hence they will soon disappear. The present little kingdom of Greece is all that is left. Brass is in itself corrosive, so the Greek Empire has gradually eaten itself away. What sublime lessons the prophets of old taught us!

The iron and clay, of which were the legs and feet, stands for the great Roman Empire, which in its day was so solid and grand with its law and order, its soldiers and statesmen. This Empire that tried the hopeless experiment of mixing clay and iron—that is, Church and State as inaugurated by Constantine. This nation that tried to fuse together Paganism and Christianity. This nation that tried to stand on two equal feet, and to encompass the whole of man, body, and spirit. Well might Daniel say of this brittle Empire that it should be partly strong and partly weak. In conscience and the empire of the soul Christ alone is King. No wonder that the Roman Empire has disappeared. The iron part is now entirely gone. The Pope and the Church of Rome foolishly arrogate to themselves to be this kingdom. They still try and believe in mixing the iron and clay—they yet claim authority in the spirit realm. Obedience to Christ and the Pope cannot be on the spiritual or clay side. No man can supremely serve two masters. On the iron side no man can be loyal to his country and the Pope at the same time. No man can serve two masters at the same time, both of which claim and demand supremacy. These things cannot be mixed. " And whereas thou sawest iron mixed with miry clay, they shall mingle themselves with the seed of men, but they shall not cleave one to another, even as iron is not mixed with clay."

How true the prophetic utterances of the prophet! The Catholics and Protestants do not mix easily, not socially not politically, nor educationally. How are we to mix freely with those who think we are heretics and damnable? How can we socially mix with a people so lordly in their claims and deficient in character as many are—a people who, when true to their profession, must be our secret or open enemies—who sink their manhood and parental claims, so as to depend upon the priest for forgiveness and on him for instruction? Thus, at the priest's command, the coming generations are divided and embittered in the fact of separate schools for Catholics and Protestants. These men of clay and lordly air, claim rights superior to the State, despising the State provision for education. Daniel said, "The dream is certain, and the interpretation thereof sure." If so, as sure as the iron part has disappeared, so will the clay.

Now a clearer view, a purer faith and greater liberty are dawning upon our Catholic friends, which is making many of them feel too manly and noble to be longer slaves to priests or Pope. Bereft of temporal power, they henceforth will have to win and fight their way, as others, on the purity of their doctrines and practice. In such a strife we can but wish them and all who love the Lord Jesus Christ, great success.

Thus in the short outline of these four kingdoms we see enough to show us that God has kept His work. How marvellous are His ways! how complete His work!

Let us now look at this stone kingdom. This fifth kingdom is as much material and political as the other four, and stands for a king, country, and people. It does not come into existence until the image is perfect. For it is while Nebuchadnezzar was looking at the image he saw the stone cut out of the mountain—its growth was gradual. Its work was to destroy this image and fill the world. As these kingdoms became weaker and smaller, it would become stronger and larger.

What king, country, and people respond to this kingdom? The answer is as easy as to find the other, if we keep our minds free from prejudice and open to truth.

First, this kingdom was of Divine origin. Second, it was small at first. Third, the more it fights the more it grows. Fourth, it breaks in pieces this image, beginning at the feet. It is, in fact, the sworn enemy of all the four kingdoms. Fifth, it is to fill the world and thus become a universal kingdom and monarchy. In this latter sense it will be a fit type of the kingdom of Christ.

DREAM IMAGE OF NEBUCHADNEZZAR. 81

Just such a kingdom as this did God repeatedly promise to Abraham and his descendants. David's throne and seed royal are to be established before Him for ever. He promised to David's throne perpetuity, and that David's seed should always be on the throne—not in the spiritual sense as some think—but naturally and actually in this world.

God promised to Israel, as a people and a kingdom, such pre-eminence in origin, power, and growth. The answer, then, is simple and plain—England, as representing the Lost Tribes of Israel, and Queen Victoria being a direct descendant from David. For she came of James VI., of Scotland—he from Bruce, and Duncan, and Malcolm, and Kenneth, and Kenneth through the Kings of Argyleshire, Alpin, and Donald, and Fergus. Then through the long line of Irish Kings from Earca to Heremon, of Tara, and he married Tea Tephi, the daughter of Zedekiah, who, through Jeremiah the prophet, had been hid from the destroying vengeance of Nebuchadnezzar. He killed all her brothers and kindred, and put out the eyes of Zedekiah and took him a captive to Babylon, where he died.

Look also at the British nation, learned as they are, yet no historian can tell who the English were originally. Sharon Turner, the best and most trustworthy on the origin of the Saxons, fails to solve the question. He traces them into Central Asia, but there he stops. They here form part of the Aryan race, speaking the Sanscrit language, from which came the Greek and Latin. And from this place and people came forth the Goths and their language, and also the Saxons and their language came to view here. The German and Saxon both seem to have come forth from the Aryan stock.

The very place the Saxons came from is the very place where the Lost Tribes were carried captive to by the King of Assyria, about 725 years before Christ, as we read in the second book of Kings, seventeenth chapter. Take the very word Saxon. This word comes from the Sanscrit: Saka Suna. Saka means

F

era, epoch, or date, and Suna means void, without. Hence the word Saxon means a people whose origin is unknown—void of date. True, Nebuchadnezzar saw no hands cutting the little stone out from the mountain. The origin of the English nation is hid because God cast away His people for a time—not for ever. It is this view of the stone kingdom that corresponds to the prophets, to history, especially to the English history.

The very island itself is insignificant, and no doubt was once joined to the continent of Europe. The formation on both sides of the English Channel—that is, on the French and English coasts, are the same—namely, chalk. The ocean in time past washed through a passage, and thus prepared a place for exiled Israel to rest in, and renew their strength.

Why should this small island and few and scattered people become so powerful, so as to sweep the sea, and dictate on land, constantly engaged in war, and though small, winning victory upon victory, and, like the stone, growing stronger and stronger, after fighting the whole of Europe, giving liberties in religion that oftentimes imperilled her safety at home, opening her ports to all the world, and venturing to compete in trade with all nations?

How came they to take India, a country of so vast an extent, so powerful, rich, and chivalrous a country, at that time composed of sixteen separate and powerful nations, speaking thirty-six different languages, and numbering in population some 200,000,000?

With all her faults, still to her the world owes much. She has stood for liberty in person and conscience. The world has little to-day which ennobles men and nations but what she has produced or aided in producing.

The right foot of the image stands for France, while the left signifies Spain. On these two feet long stood Rome, as all know. When these two feet were broken, then soon followed the downfall of Rome as an Empire, and as they are conquered for Jesus, so will the empire of Rome, as a Church, fall.

In the year 1346 took place the battle of Cressey, led by Edward III, Then the little stone fell on the right foot, and since then it has fallen on that same foot victoriously 218 times. On the left foot, Spain, thirty-five times. All this time this stone has been growing. In 1665 the English, under General Penn, took Jamaica, and every four years since they have added a colony. Now that little stone bears rule over fifty-five colonies, one empire—namely, India—and one dominion, Canada. And yet, mighty as England was, she could not subdue the American provinces, feeble and scattered colonists as they were. Then they sought to fight against Providence. Old Jacob blessed the sons of Joseph. Ephraim, and Manasseh, and then predicted their destiny, saying of Manasseh, "He also shall become a people, and he also shall be great; but truly his younger brother shall be greater than he, and his seed shall become a multitude of nations." So they are; and so Manasseh is a great people in the American nation.

This stone, cut out of the mountain, has much to do and destroy; it is still watching the head of gold. Israel and Babylon are still face to face. Greece will first disappear, although England is trying to revive it. Next, Persia will go, then Babylon, or head of gold. Russia will have grown to giant-like proportions, and will finally measure swords with England. The stone will win. England will then move her royal residence and throne to Jerusalem. Every country and province may then be independent, like Canada, but federated to the central government. Ireland will then be free, yes, doubly free—free from Rome and free from England as a State, but still federated to the central government. It is thus this stone will fill the earth. America will federate, the central government will be destroyed. State rights increase. These are some of the things suggested and taught by this vision.

LITTLE HORN AND TURKEY.
DISCOURSE VIII.

The Turks, the Ishmaelites—England and Russia to Partition the Mahommedan Empire—Why England Sympathises with Turkey.

"And out of one of them came forth a little horn, which waxed exceeding great, toward the South, and toward the East, and toward the pleasant land."—Daniel viii. 9.

NEBUCHADNEZZAR had a dream, in which he saw a great metallic image of human form. The head of gold stood for Babylon; the silver arms and breast for Persia; the brass belly and thighs for Greece; the iron legs and feet of iron and clay for Rome. To all this we find history has faithfully and beautifully responded.

A few years after this we find that Daniel has a dream, which is interpreted to him by an angel. From it we learn that the ten toes symbolised ten kingdoms which were to arise out of the Roman Empire.

In the chapter from which we take our text, we are introduced into the secrets of a vision which Daniel had. The place of the vision is on the banks of the River Ulai, in the province of Elam, and in the gorgeous palace of Shushan—a place and palace made famous and familiar to us by the doings of King Ahasuerus and Queen Esther. In other words, the scene is changed from the palace of Babylon to the palace of Persia.

In this vision, Persia is typified by a ram, the two horns of which represented Persia and Media, and they formed one Empire at this time, under the powerful rule and reign of Cyrus, who, coming from the East, pushed his conquests "Westward, and Northward, and Southward." "The two horns were high; but one was higher than the other, and the higher came up last." From history we know that Media conquered Persia, and we know, also, that finally Persia gained ascendancy, so that the higher came up last, and is even in existence to-day as the small kingdom of Persia; but Media has long since disappeared.

While the seer Daniel was considering, behold an he-goat came from the West. This goat had a notable horn between his eyes. Horn generally symbolises power; here it symbolises a king of peculiar power, Daniel tells us. Goat-like, it bounded over the earth rapidly, pushing and goring its adversaries. Can any one at all acquainted with history fail to see how fitly and grandly this description of the goat forecasts the origin and progress of the Greek Empire?

Substitute Alexander the Great for the notable horn, and you at once mate history and this vision. Surely God has not left Himself without witnesses. "Then the magicians said unto Pharaoh, This is the finger of God." So we may freely say unto the historians and students of history, Truly in these things we see the finger of God.

Could any historian describe more faithfully and accurately the invasions, conquests, and victories of Alexander the Great, especially his assault on the Persians? How marvellous and simple the description by Daniel: "And he came to the ram that had two horns (Persia), which I had seen standing before the river, and ran unto him in the fury of his power; and I saw him come close unto the ram, and he was moved with choler against him, and smote the ram, and brake his two horns; and there was no power in the ram to stand before him, but he cast him down to the ground, and stamped upon him; and there was none that could deliver the ram out of his hand."

And with the same majestic simplicity we have the downfall of Alexander and the division of his Empire described. Listen! "Therefore the he-goat waxed very great; and when he was strong the great horn was broken; and for it came up four notable ones toward the four winds of heaven."

To fully understand the sacred writer here, you must call to mind a little of history, more and better, for all knowledge only aids us the better and better to read the Bible.

What beast, save the goat, could characterise Alexander and his reign? He was the son of Philip of Macedon, born 356 B.C., and died in 323. He began his reign at twenty years of age, and closed it in twelve years and eight months. No man in the same time ever fought so many battles, won so many victories, and subdued so many people. No man, before or since, ever ruled over so many people and such a kingdom. Queen Victoria is in these things his only rival. But with his sudden death the fruits of his victories are re-distributed. His Empire was divided into four parts; the four Diadochi were his successors. What lessons may men and nations learn by studying the prophecies!

"For prophecy came not in old time by the will of man; but holy men of God spake as they were moved by the Holy Ghos ;" and unto this sure word of prophecy we do well to take heed, as unto a light that shineth in a dark place. "Knowing this first, that no prophecy of the Scripture is of any private interpretation" (2 Peter i. 20). As naturally as nature responds to the seasons, so will providence to prophecy. We can discern spring-time, summer, autumn, and winter. The garden will reveal to us winter as distinct from summer, so in interpreting prophecy we must always look for an agreement between providence and the world. As naturally as the goat symbolises Alexander, so will providence in national history respond. Winter, with its winds, storms, and frost; with its leafless trees and desolate gardens, proclaims, beyond a doubt, which season of the four is bearing rule. Such a thing cannot be of private interpretation; and prophecy, when fulfilled, is as easy seen, and is not of private interpretation. A man is as foolish in forging prophecy as one would be in trying to forge winter by putting artificial leaves on trees, and flowers on bushes.

The thing is easily known if we exercise our reason. In this line of thought we are sorry to note that men have more faith than reason; hence the blunderings of prophetic writers, and the leaders of Adventism and Millenarianism. Prophecy unfulfilled commands and demands our faith—much more faith than reason, for it is impossible to see how some things can come to pass, but if they are subjects of prophecy they surely will, whether we understand them or not. A prophecy fulfilled, however, appeals more to reason than faith, for if fulfilled, it can readily be demonstrated.

As naturally as the female and male birds know each other and mate together, so will events and prophecy. This kind of argument Isaiah uses: "Seek ye out of the Book of the Lord and read; no one of these shall fail, none shall want her mate, for My mouth it hath commanded, and His Spirit it hath gathered them" (Isa. xxxiv. 16). I charge you to beware of prophetic dentists who put false teeth in the mouth of prophecy; who by their haste and impatience forestall prophecy and weaken men's faith instead of strengthening it. Prophetic evidence is very strong evidence, both for the Christian and the infidel.

Some will fail to be convinced when prophecy is fulfilled. Jew-like, they will blind their eyes and shut their ears to the evidences and voice of fulfilled prophecy. The entire career of our Lord Jesus Christ was foretold and mapped out by the Old Testament writers. Moses declared His family; Micah the place of His birth; Isaiah the virginity of His mother; Zechariah His triumphant entry into Jerusalem; David His life, resurrection, and ascension, with many other kinds of evidence of a detailed and general character; yet the Jews, who claimed to be well versed in the Old Testament, rejected Christ. Keep these things in mind while we now consider the text more directly.

You remember that out of the great kingdom there came up

four notable ones, and out of one of them came forth a little horn, which waxed exceeding great toward the South, East, and pleasant land, or land of Palestine. Now this horn is not to be confounded with the little horn of the fourth kingdom spoken of in chapter vii., for that horn might justly be called the eleventh toe horn, as it comes into existence after the ten-toe kingdoms. The little horn of the text is explained in verse 23 to be a king of fierce countenance. He was to appear in the latter time. It will be interesting for us to ascertain what king, people, and country this little horn stands for. Daniel has given us a very vivid picture of the king. He is to be of fierce countenance, to understand dark sentences, to stand up in power and might, not however in his own power; he will claim to be appointed and authorised of God, and will pretend to rule in God's name; he will destroy wonderfully even the mighty of the world and the holy people; he will be very prosperous and practical, giving a great impetus to trade. By means of his prosperity he will become proud and strong, and will destroy many. He will actually stand up in place of Jesus—Prince of princes. But finally he will be broken without a hand. Thus, you see, Daniel gives us twelve special features of his person and reign. Without doubt the mate of these descriptions will be found on the person of Mahommed, and his successors in religion Mahommedanism, and in people and country the Turks and Turkey.

Mahommed had his religion and himself recognised about the year 622 at Mecca. From that time and place he went forth to waste and to destroy. As his religion prevailed, so he subdued the country or territory. He united in himself the rights and prerogatives of king, priest, and prophet, making it obligatory upon his followers to prepare a way and enforce his religion by the sword. He was indeed a king of fierce countenance. Thus sprang Mahommedanism and the Turkish nation into existence. As a people, they are chiefly the descendants of Esau and Ishmael. If one desires to know the history and final destiny of this people, let him study the prophetic utterances concerning Esau and Ishmael. They are the descendants of Abraham, and so they very naturally fall into the prophetic line.

The Hungarians came from this family through Lot. The Poles and Magyars are from Moab and Ammon. These things being so, it is no wonder the Hungarians and Turks should sympathise, nor that England should have a liking for Turks, England being the Ten Lost Tribes of Israel. Alliance and sympathy between England and Turkey has a deeper root and meaning than some are willing to admit. Turkey, however, as a distinct empire, is nearly at an end. The recognition of the Ten Lost Tribes, and their restoration with the Jews to Palestine, is connected with the downfall of Turkey. "Saviours are to come up on Mount Zion to judge the Mount of Esau, and the kingdom shall be the Lord's" (Obad.).

How clearly speaks Obadiah again when he says, "How are the things of Esau searched out? how are his hidden things sought up? All the men of thy confederacy have brought thee even to the border; the men that were at peace with thee have deceived thee, and prevailed against thee; they that eat thy bread have laid a wound under thee; there is none understanding in him. Shall I not in that day, saith the Lord, even destroy the wise men out of Edom, and understanding out of the Mount of Esau?"

These are the latter times of the king of fierce countenance. Hear Daniel inquiring of the angel in this vision, "How long shall be the vision concerning the daily sacrifice and the transgression of desolation, to give both the sanctuary and the host to be trodden under foot? And he said unto me, Unto two thousand and three hundred days." These days are generally allowed to stand for years. If so, Jerusalem was destroyed 70 A.D. The time Daniel saw this vision was about 490 B.C.; take

70 from this leaves 420. From 2,300 take 420, and we have 1,880. "Then shall the sanctuary be cleansed." What means this? It means that Jerusalem will recur back again into the hands of the Jews and Israel. Christ said that the Jews "Should fall by the edge of the sword, and be led away captive into all nations; and Jerusalem shall be trodden down of the Gentiles, until the times of the Gentiles be fulfilled" (Luke xxi. 24).

Now we know the Jews did fall by the sword when the Romans took Jerusalem. Second, we know they were scattered among the nations. Third, Jerusalem has been trodden under foot—so much so, that Christians have not been permitted to stand on Mount Zion, where now stands the Mosque of Ommar. And this is the city of the great King. This is Mount Zion, from which is yet to go forth the law. This is Jerusalem that God promises to yet again make the chief place of the earth. "Arise, shine, for thy light is come, and the glory of the Lord is risen upon thee." When, we ask, will the fulness of the Gentiles come in? We answer, Soon. Think of what God has taught us in His Word. We, as the Lost Tribes, have indeed been ignorant of our origin and destiny. "For I would not, brethren, that ye should be ignorant of this mystery, lest ye should be wise in your own conceits, that blindness in part is happened to Israel, until the fulness of the Gentiles be come in" (Rom. xi. 25). This time is nicely pointed out by John in Rev. xi. 2: "But the court which is without the temple leave out, and measure it not; for it is given unto the Gentiles, and the holy city shall they tread under foot forty and two months;" or, as explained in the following verse, a thousand two hundred and three-score days. Accepting a day for a year again, and we have 1,260 years. Taking Mahommed power to date from 622, or about, then 622 and 1,260 make 1,882. Now just as sure as Jerusalem is now trodden under foot, as certainly will it be free.

"Awake, awake; put on thy strength, O Zion; put on thy beautiful garments, O Jerusalem, the holy city; for henceforth there shall no more come into thee the uncircumcised and the unclean. Shake thyself from the dust; arise and sit down, O Jerusalem; loose thyself from the bands of thy neck, O captive daughter of Zion" (Isa. lii. 1, 2).

England is appointed of God to take possession of Palestine and restore Jerusalem. The present European Congress will but further the design. God has told us through Isaiah that He will lay vengeance upon Edom by the hand of Israel. The work of the Congress is all cut and dried for them; just as, near two years ago, we pointed out to you the war, its course and the parties thereto, and the results, so now we can forecast the results of the coming Congress. Russia and England will both gain; Turkey will be the loser. The many days of the vision of Daniel are now gone; the time is nearly up.

"For Zion's sake will I not hold My peace, and for Jerusalem's sake I will not rest, until the righteousness thereof go forth as brightness, and the salvation thereof as a lamp that burneth; and the Gentiles shall see thy righteousness, and all kings thy glory." It is the duty of the watchmen of Zion to discern the signs of the times and become obedient unto heavenly instruction. "Ye that make mention of the Lord, keep not silence, and give Him no rest till He establish, and till He make Jerusalem a praise in the earth" (Isa. lxii. 1, 2, 6, 7).

LITTLE HORN AND ANTI-CHRIST.
Discourse IX.

Prophetic Wonders—Twenty Marks of the Monster—The Berlin Congress — Anti-Christs Many — Mistakes by Writers.

"I considered the horns, and behold! there came up among them another little horn, before whom there were three of the first horns plucked up by the roots; and behold! in this horn were eyes like the eyes of man, and a mouth speaking great things."—Daniel vii. 8.

In the visions and dream recorded by Daniel in this chapter we have the same subject-matter as that contained in the dream of Nebuchadnezzar of the metallic image. In this the subject is carried further into the future, bringing to view some new items of interest, under different symbols and more of detail. The four kingdoms of the metallic image are in this dream presented by the symbolism of four beasts. Babylon by a lion which had eagle's wings, setting forth the strength and swiftness of the same. Persia by a bear raised up on one side. Persia at this time was composed of Media as well, but the one-sided position of the bear denotes the dying out of Media and the continuance of Persia. The same idea is conveyed in the eighth chapter and third verse: "The ram had two horns, and one was higher than the other, and the higher came up last." Media was a kingdom before Persia, but Persia was to survive Media; all this history confirms. After the Medo-Persian Empire declined, Persia surviving, held on to Babylon, Lydia, and Egypt—that is, when the bear was raised up on one side, it held in its mouth three ribs, and was strong for a time.

The Macedonian Empire Daniel saw under the type of a leopard, which had on its back four wings of a fowl; the beast also had four heads. Babylon was represented by two wings, but it is very fitting that Alexander and his empire should have four wings, for no conqueror ever flew so fast over the earth as this same monarch. In the metallic image he is represented by brass, in this by a leopard, and in the one we noticed in Discourse VII., by the goat. How wonderfully appropriate are these symbolisms! The four heads of this leopard stand for the four kingdoms into which the Macedonian Empire was divided on the death of Alexander—namely, first, Egypt under Ptolemy; second, Syria under Antigonus; third, Asia Minor under Lysimachus; fourth, Greece under Cassander. These four kings were the four leading generals of Alexander.

The fourth beast of this vision is a nondescript; for among all the animal creation there could not be found one that could suitably represent Rome. But one was made for the purpose, combining in itself all that is fierce and terrible. "And behold a fourth beast, dreadful and terrible, and strong exceedingly; and it had great iron teeth; it devoured and brake in pieces, and stamped the residue with the feet of it; and it was diverse from all the beasts that were before it; and it had ten horns." Its teeth were of iron, and its claws of brass. What a monster! The other beasts faithfully represented their respective kingdoms, and so did this. What a record! What a counterpart we have in history of this beast! "Tell it not in Gath, publish it not in the streets of Askelon," lest the Pagan rejoice, and the heathen mock at us, and the infidel triumph over us. Blot out from Time's record the 24th of August, 1572. Let not our children learn the name of St. Bartholomew, for fear they should despise Christianity. Quench the flames of Smithfield, destroy the Inquisition, and divorce Christianity from such a kingdom, from such a beast. Thank Heaven! the beast is dying; its teeth are worn to the very gum by the gnawings of centuries; its claws are not now sharp, so it cannot now crush the innocent, as in days gone by, nor tear with its brass claw the weak. Though the beast is growing old and weaker, yet let us remember that its death struggle is yet to come. The beast has been wounded, but this shall only serve to intensify its rage. To be forewarned is to be forearmed, if we are wise.

This beast, Daniel tells us, had ten horns, and these horns are ten kings—that is, kingdoms—that shall arise. Just here we may reasonably ask whether these ten kingdoms are yet in existence, and the answer is, No. Some of them may be ; of course they are in existence, as was General Grant before the war, but not yet distinct or assigned their special work or place. The time, however, for them all to appear is near at hand. Of this we may rest satisfied, when once they are all in existence, we will have no difficulty in knowing them. Prophecy unfulfilled is alway more difficult to interpret than when it is fulfilling or fulfilled. We have no doubt but some of these horns are in existence, and from what we can glean from prophecy and history, some are not yet in their proper place.

The special province of prophecy is to prepare us for what is coming. Searching into prophecy enables us to forecast the future with tolerable certainty, just as the scientist can tolerably forecast the weather by studying the laws, forces, and inclinations of nature. So the Christian student, by studying prophecy, Providence, and history, and comparing them, can know much of what is coming. On the Divine side all prophecy is certain, but on the human it can only be approximated. Prophecy furnishes the strongest kind of evidence in favour of the existence of God—inspiration of the Scriptures and Providence. The Lord Himself calls our attention to this kind of evidence frequently in the Bible. " Produce your cause, saith the Lord ; bring forth your strong reasons, saith the King of Jacob. Let them bring them forth and show us what shall happen ; let them show the former things what they be, that we may consider them, and know the latter end of them ; or declare us things for to come " (Isa. xli. 21, 22).

Prophecy does not interfere with the coming to pass of an event, or suppress man's freedom, no more than the man at

Washington, who gives us the weather probabilities, makes the weather or regulates nature. Even when men know the sequence of a thing they oftentimes persist in doing it. The soldiers who wrangled at the cross about the dividing of the garments of the crucified One, thought little, and cared less for prophecy; but when they came to the Saviour's vest, they fell into the line of prophecy, for at once they cast lots for that, all of which had been fore-written for hundreds of years. Run and tell that young man that the place he is entering is the way of death. Tell him that the air is foul, that the furniture and painted humanity are all gotten up to deceive. Tell him that in a few years he will repent ever having seen such a place. And what is your reward? It is that you are laughed at, and esteemed as one that interferes, and told to mind your own business. The young man is free and self-confident. Look in a few years for that same young man, and you shall find him a terrible example of fulfilled prophecy. Diseased, worn, weak, and weary, he cries in the anguish of soul for his folly. "And thou mourn at the last, when thy flesh and thy body are consumed, and say, How have I hated instruction and my heart despised reproof?" (Prov. v. 11, 12).

The famous European Congress which met in Berlin, we foresaw would meet near three years ago, and told you the conditions under which it would be called. In the dark days of the past did we not repeat to you our faith, as fostered from Prophecy, that England could not go to war? Many of you, and persons in different parts of the country, advised me by letter, when the telegraph despatches came crowding and threatening, that I had so said. This intention was to break my faith, or at least to remind me that I had not spoken correctly. What now! who is right? The Congress completed a prophetic period. After it was over, new scenery appeared, and a new act came upon the stage. But more of this by-and-bye.

Among the results of this Congress will be an enlargement of England's power over Turkey and Egypt. For England must possess Constantinople, because to Israel it is promised that he shall possess the gates of his enemies, and this is one of the finest gates in the world. Palestine will come into the hands of England, and be opened up for the return of the Jews, who, when the time comes, will go in multitudes, and the Lost Tribes representatively. "I will take you one of a city, and two of a family, and I will bring you to Zion" (Jer. iii. 14). In a few years men will understand why, in this country, as well as in England, people are hunting up their genealogy, and by tradition, history, and heraldry, trying to ascertain of what family they are. The re-settlement of Palestine by God's chosen people, the Lost Tribes, no one can deny who reads and believes the Bible. Hanging upon the fulfilment of this great fact are many other prophecies and events, which are of great interest to the Church and the world.

1st. The ten-toed kingdom must be formed. These kings are to form an alliance with the beast, or Church of Rome, as representative of this beast. "And the ten horns which thou sawest are ten kings, which have received no kingdom as yet, but receive power as kings one hour with the beast. These have one mind, and shall give their power and strength unto the beast" (Rev. xvii. 12). Thus strengthened, the beast will make war with the saints, or chosen; but it will be her final struggle, for in struggling she will die. These ten kings will forsake her.

2nd. Anti-Christ has to appear after the settlement of Palestine. Anti-Christ is represented by the other little horn spoken of in the text. This little horn is to come forth from one of the ten horns. He, too, will ally with the beast. The subject of anti-Christ is a very interesting one; on it, men have written and speculated much and wildly. In studying a subject of this kind, we should first ascertain the Scripture teachings on it, then look for the preparative signs in the Church and world, and finally, for the counterpart, which, once in existence, no one can fail to recognise. The time, person, and work of Anti-Christ have been very clearly set forth in the Old and New Testaments, especially by Isaiah, in the fourteenth chapter and twelfth to sixteenth verses; by Daniel in the seventh and eleventh chapters, under the symbolism of this little horn; by Paul in second Thessalonians, second chapter and first to twelfth verses; also by John in Revelation, thirteenth chapter and nineteenth chapter and twentieth verse, besides many other references.

Of Anti-Christ the early Christian fathers had different views. 1st. Some thought that he would be Satan assuming the appearance of a man. 2nd. Some thought he would be a hybrid, the offspring of Satan by a harlot; of this opinion were Lactantius and Sulspitius. 3rd. Hilary, Jerome, and others, thought he would be Satan incarnated. 4th. Chrysostom, Theopolact, and Theodoret thought he would be a real man under the influence of the devil. This latter view we accept as being the nearest to the Scripture teaching. In the Scriptures he goes by the names of Lucifer, man of sin, son of perdition, and that wicked one. Now all these names are indictative of some special feature of his character. Man of sin points out the intensity of the person in wickedness. As some time ago a man was called "the wickedest man in New York," so Anti-Christ will be called "the man of sin," having been the greatest sinner of human kind.

From the Scriptures we find that he will be characterised by some twenty peculiarities. These we will just enumerate: a cunning seducer, a vile impostor, a bold blasphemer, a great tyrant, a wonderful organiser and diplomatist; hence he will readily make alliances with other kings and strengthen himself; a pretentious and hypocritical Communist; dividing his lands, money, and treasure among the people; he will be very ambitious and aspiring, doing or being anything so he may gain his point;

G

he will be very self-willed; he will be very boastful, speaking great words; he will be very cruel, not heeding the plea of woman; he will be very sacreligious, sitting in the temple of God—that is, the new temple, built by the returned Jews—and actually claim to be God ; he will be a scientific spiritualist, able to work miracles, even to bring fire down from the clouds; he will be very powerful by his alliance, apparent generosity, and scientific deception; he will be a great liar, making treaties and breaking them whenever it suits him; he will be very wicked, guilty of all manner of crime; his reign will be short as a king, only about three-and-a-half years. Before this he will have been a man of power and position. He will suddenly be destroyed in the time of a fearful uprising of the people ; he will remain unburied in the streets of Jerusalem for a time, then, finally, his remains will be burned up. These and many other facts inspiration furnish us beforehand of this most wonderful character.

Against this person our Saviour warned the Jews and all the Church, but especially the Jews, and He did so for special reasons, which will appear hereafter in this discourse. Christ said, " I am come in My Father's name, and ye receive Me not; if another shall come in his own name, him ye shall receive." At the time of Anti-Christ's death there will be raging a fearful war, and coincident with this war there will be another Saint Bartholomew massacre in several of the ten-toed kingdoms. The beast and Anti-Christ are to be destroyed about the same time. It will be the last plot of the Jesuits, who are hounding to death poor Leo XIII. A glimpse of that time the Saviour showed to His disciples, when He said: " For then shall be great tribulation, such as was not since the beginning of the world, to this time, no, nor ever shall be; and except those days should be shortened, there should no flesh be saved; but for the elect's sake those days shall be shortened. Then, if any man shall say unto you, Lo ! here is Christ, or there, believe it not for there shall arise false Christs, and false prophets, and shall show great signs and wonders, insomuch that if it were possible, they shall deceive the very elect. Behold! I have told you before" (Matt. xxiv. 21—25).

What a warning the Saviour gave the Jews, but how little have they and the Church heeded it! In the second century appeared the famous Bar Cochebas, with his thousands of followers, who in his final struggle was slain with some sixty thousand of his adherents. Also think of Antiochus Epiphanes and his terrible delusions, the thousands and tens of thousands who flocked to his standard. So marvellous was this delusion, that many have actually made him out to be Anti-Christ, but those who thus reason take the shadow for the substance, and do violence to all true Scripture exegesis. Antiochus Epiphanes could not be Anti-Christ, for he was out of time, and meets but few of the special conditions of Anti-Christ. History records the appearance of not less than twenty-five Anti-Christs, or persons who have claimed to be the Messiah of the Jews. How unbelief exposes a man or a people!

Some have laboured to make it appear that Mahommed was Anti-Christ, but with all his badness, he is not bad enough to be Anti-Christ. He reviled not God, he never sat in His temple, he did not die in Jerusalem. He had an honourable burial.

Some have tried to prove that Romanism and the Pope were Anti-Christ, but this cannot be, you will see at a glance. The beast has its own character; that was long ago written out by the prophets, and up to the present time it has filled in the outlines with a marvellous minuteness. In these things many good and wise men have erred in making prophecies fit certain persons, and nations, and times, instead of waiting for these things to fit on to prophecy. Let us not be prophetic forgers. Let no one deceive you in these matters. Adventism, Millerism, Shakerism, Spiritualism, are untimely excesses. As systems they are, as yet, out of place. The subject of Anti-Christ, as to who he will be, and when he will appear, I shall deal with in my next discourse. May the good Lord guide us into the ways of truth and peace.

ANTI-CHRIST AND LITTLE HORN.
Discourse X.

Second Discourse on the Monster—Who He Will be and His Name—How he Will Obtain Power—Trouble for Germany, France, and Russia—Communism—Romanism—Shakers—Matthias, Westchester Prophet.

"Let no man deceive you by any means; for that day shall not come, except there come a falling away first, and that man of sin be revealed, the son of perdition; who opposeth and exalteth himself above all that is called God, or that is worshipped, so that he, as God, sitting in the temple of God, showing himself that he is God."—2 Thess. ii. 3, 4.

WE may reasonably ask why Paul gave the Thessalonians this caution, and the answer will appear at once if we read his first epistle to this people. There you will find Paul writing to them about the second coming of Christ, which writing the Thessalonians had evidently misunderstood, and this misunderstanding was working mischief among them. They had false hopes and expectations. Their faith, instead of exciting them to holy activity in Church and State, had begun to paralyse all their efforts. "For this we say unto you by the word of the Lord, that *we* which are alive and remain unto the coming of the Lord shall not prevent them which are asleep; for the

Lord Himself shall descend from heaven with a shout, with the voice of the archangel and with the trump of God; and the dead in Christ shall rise first (that is, before Christ descends); then *we* which are alive and remain shall be caught up together with them in the clouds, to meet the Lord in the air; and so shall *we* ever be with the Lord" (1 Thess. iv. 15—17). It was the frequent use of the pronoun "we" that had confused them —*we* who remain, *we* who are alive. The Thessalonians had inferred from this that the second coming of Christ would take place in their day. Hence, to correct this impression Paul thus writes in his second epistle. The two verses preceding the text show us Paul's intent. "Now we beseech you, brethren, by the coming of our Lord Jesus Christ, and by our gathering together unto Him, that ye be not soon shaken in mind, or be troubled, neither by spirit, nor by word, nor by letter as from us, as that the day of Christ is at hand." Then comes in the text, "Let no man deceive you," &c.

In reasoning on such important subjects as Anti-Christ, resurrection, and second coming of Christ, we should always be mindful of the Scriptural order. When we sit down to take dinner, we follow the order that custom has prescribed—soup, fish, meats, and dessert. Children, however, if let alone, would reverse this order by beginning with the dessert first. So with many Christians, they reverse the order of things as laid down in the Bible. They make Christ to come before Anti-Christ, and Anti-Christ to come before the Jews, and Ten Lost Tribes are gathered together again and settled after their first estate in Palestine. The Millerites could neither have deceived themselves nor others had they taken knowledge of the relation of things. The Jews and Lost Tribes had not been gathered together then, the temple had not been built in Jerusalem, as described in the last chapter of Ezekiel, neither had Anti-Christ appeared. But such was the folly of men then, and not less now than then. Four-fifths of the prophecies of the Bible refer to the history of Judah and Israel in their own land, their captivity and return in the latter day. Still men take one-fifth and confuse themselves and everybody else. They have brought the prophets and prophecy into bad repute by ignorantly or wilfully interpreting the same.

We freely avow now that the prophecy fulfilling at present is the finding of the Lost Ten Tribes, then their union with the Jews, then their restoration to Palestine, then after being settled there for some time, the Jews, as Jews, having built their new temple, and having established the Mosaic temple service again, and the Lost Tribes as Christians, then and there we may look for Anti-Christ—not before. Not for the sake of boasting, and yet without fear, we freely invite ministers or laymen anywhere to disprove these facts, and to such we will respond cheerfully if asked for further proof. The Lost Tribes, we believe, are come to light, and may be found in the Saxon race chiefly as represented in this country and Great Britain. If this be so, then we may look for the preparatory signs in Providence and nations, and, thank Heaven, these are at hand and in accord with the Divine Word.

In Nebuchadnezzar's metallic image we saw Rome symbolised by the legs, composed of iron and clay. We saw, also, that the little stone cut out of the mountain began its destructive assault on the image, by striking the feet; these it would first break, so Rome politically has disappeared. The ten toes, however, symbolised ten kings or kingdoms that were to arise in the latter day, or at the time of the end. These ten kingdoms are also symbolised in Daniel's dream by ten horns that came out of the head of the nondescript animal that stood for Rome. It is out of one of these ten horns that another little horn grows, having eyes like a man and a mouth speaking great things— that is, Anti-Christ. It is at once plain, then, that ere Anti-Christ can appear, these ten kindoms must be formed.

How, when, and where will these ten kingdoms be formed?

ANTI-CHRIST AND LITTLE HORN.

The clay part of Rome is still alive, and is designated by Daniel, and by John in Revelation, under the name of beast; and here you need to be careful, for the word beast is sometimes given to Anti-Christ, so as not to confound it with the word beast when it stands for the Romish Church. They will be formed out of Spain, Italy, France, and part of Austria. Edom, Moab, and the sons of Ammon in Austria, are to be free—that is, the Poles, Magyars, and Hungarians. The setting up of these ten kingdoms will begin in France by a revolution.

By the doctrine of infallibility, these countries are claimed by Rome, and wedded to her, and this doctrine of infallibility makes a divorce impossible. Rome waits only her time to reclaim her supposed own. And this doctrine of infallibility will make it a holy war, hence good and true Catholics everywhere will be obliged to sustain the same by their money, or presence, or prayers. This, to many of our Catholic friends, will sound strange. But this they know, if such an emergency ever does arise—they cannot well fight against the infallible Church—between commands and duties, they will readily prefer the Pope and Church to king and country.

The Jesuits are now, and have long been, preparing for such an event: they expect it. By their plottings and intrigues they will again, as many times before, involve the Church in war. They are busy sowing the seeds of discord. In past time both the Church itself and nations have banished these crafty fellows from their pale and country. The United States alone, of the nations of the earth, is the only one that has not so done. But even among us they are plotting and manœuvring to such an extent that it will not be long before America will be tested and tried on this same subject.

Among the preparatory signs of the coming of Anti-Christ we have Communism, which is destined to spread. In Europe it will unsettle every throne but one—that is, Israel, England. We fear that neither the Church nor State comprehend the terrible power that is thus quietly organising in this and other lands. It is this uprising of the Communists and intriguing of the Jesuits in our own land, that will call General Grant once more to the front, as we pointed out to you months ago. The recent European Congress resulted in patching up a temporary peace between Russia, England, and Turkey. A place will be provided for the Duke of Edinburgh, who, having married the Czar's daughter, will enable the two Powers to agree. He may not be the first prince, still he and his seed are to find a kingdom in that place. Russia will be willing for England to have Constantinople, and exercise a provisional protectorate over Turkey, with a view of strengthening his daughter's chances. England will thus come peaceably in possession of Palestine.

Germany, being tied to both the Russian and English thrones by blood and marriage, will also freely consent. Besides, Germany is going to pass through a severe trial. The old Emperor will soon die, and also Bismark, then a new prince will advise the new king, new counsel, and new blood, near and on the throne. Germany will become a prey to eternal strife, fanned by the discontented Catholics of the Empire, that number some 15,000,000, and weakened by the Communistic elements. Not much longer can Germany bear the strain of her immense army and enormous taxes in consequence.

Russia also will have all she can do to stay the desire for reform, and the claims of the Nihilists or Communists. Thus will Providence prepare His people's way back to Palestine.

If God promises once He does so fifty times, that He will restore Israel and Judah to their own land. To this one thing all Providence is concentrating, and this is the key that unseals prophecy and Providence. "And I will cause the captivity of Judah and the captivity of Israel to return, and will build them as at the first" (Jer. xxxiii. 7). They will form a free province, electing their own rulers and governors. They will be quite

ANTI-CHRIST AND LITTLE HORN. 105

democratic, doing away with all titles, being the children of the Lord, "And the nobles shall be of themselves, and their governor shall proceed from the midst of them" (Jer. xxx. 21); or, as stated by Isaiah, chap. i., verse 26, "And I will restore thy judges as at the first, and thy counsellors as at the beginning; afterward thou shalt be called, The city of righteousness, the faithful city." Thus they will be a free province, managing their own affairs under the patronage and protection of England. Now it is this freedom that will open the door and prepare the way for Anti-Christ. He will be elected governor because of his supposed superiority in manners, science, and benevolence. He will appear as a lamb at first, according to John, but once in power his true character will appear. He will be a great scientist, and in the eyes and faith of the multitude he will be able to work miracles—to bring, scientifically, fire down from heaven. So clever will he be that he will deceive some of the very elect.

Before his election he will have been a man of great power and influence. Once in power he will contrive to centre all power and interests in himself. He will pander to the Communists—to the Romish Church—to the scientific infidels of the day. In this feature he will draw heavily on the Germans, and create quite a sympathy in England and this country. "For some of them of understanding shall fall, to try them, and to purge, and to make them white even to the time of the end" (Dan. xi. 35).

The Scriptures having pointed out the special features of his character, we see that many of these features are already in the world. This is Anti-Christ. This is the spirit of Anti-Christ. And when God withdraws His restraining power, Anti-Christ will embody all these forces and characteristics in himself. And all men having these features will sympathise with him, and aid him. God alone is now keeping back and down this spirit of Anti-Christ until His own chosen time. "And now ye know what withholdeth, that he might be revealed in his time; for the mystery of iniquity doth already work, only he who now letteth will let until he be taken out of the way (that is, till God withdraws Himself), and then shall that wicked be revealed."

Anti-Christ means one opposed to Christ. Also it means one opposed to Christ, and yet desires to be Christ—who wishes to be received as Christ. And when the time comes, he will be received by many. The Jews will be looking for and expecting the coming of their Messiah, hence many of these will be deceived. Many radical Adventists and Millenarians will accept him, because they are in haste in their expectations: many of these will follow him. Indeed, the whole world seems ripe to furnish him a quota. But who will he be? Answer: He will be a French Jew, who will intermarry into the Bonaparte family. His title will be Napoleon I. of Palestine. This word Napoleon, resolved into Greek equivalents, is equal to Apollyon, and as a number stands for 666. " Here is wisdom. Let him that hath understanding count the number of the beast, for it is the number of a man; and his number is six hundred three-score and six " (Rev. viii. 18).

Christ, when warning the Jews of Anti-Christ, said, "I am come in My Father's name, and ye receive Me not; if another shall come in his own name, him ye will receive." Here, and in other discourses, we have to content ourselves at many points with mere statements, for to defend every point would take too long a time, and would not suit our purpose. It is our desire in all these discourses to incite you to study, to teach you to examine for yourselves; to prepare you against being unduly led away by Adventism, Communism, or Infidelity; to give you an interest in Providence and history. Do you ask if any will be led away by such a false pretender? We answer, Yes— unless humanity undergoes some radical change. Take a few instances:—

Our Shaker friends believed in Mother Ann Lee. This woman in 1770, while living in Manchester, England, pretended to have a special revelation from Heaven, making known unto her that she was the female side of Christ—as Jesus was the revelation of the male side. As Eve was taken out of Adam, the female principle separated from the male, so she was separated from Christ. This, and much that is curious, do these sincere, honest, and industrious people believe.

Take another example, nearer home, and of which some of you are cognizant, having known the pretender and many of his duped followers. We refer to Matthias, the prophet of Westchester County. This pretended lord began his labours in Albany, N.Y., in 1830. First he taught himself to be God's high priest, then the Saviour, then he claimed to be God. On being asked where he was from, he would answer: "I am a traveller, and my legal residence is Zion Hill, Westchester County, New York State. I am a Jewish teacher and priest of the Most High God, saying and doing all that I do, under oath, by virtue of my having subscribed to all the covenants that God hath made with man from the beginning up to this time. I am chief high priest of the Jews of the order of Melchizedec, being the last chosen of the twelve apostles, and the first in the resurrection which is at the end of 2,300 years from the birth of Mahhomed, which terminates in 1830. I am now denouncing judgment on the Gentiles, and that judgment is to be executed in this age."

He appeared in fine pontifical robes, with a rule six feet long in his right hand; with this he was to measure off God's holy city. In his left hand he had a two-edged sword. Underneath his pontifical robe he had a rich olive broadcloth cloak, lined and faced with silk and velvet; besides, he wore a brown frock coat, with several stars on each breast, with a splendid gold star on the left. His belt was of white cloth, fastened by a golden clasp, and surmounted with an eagle. He wore a cocked hat of black beaver, trimmed with green, the rear angle being surmounted by the golden symbol of glory.

He moved from Albany to New York, and here succeeded most wonderfully, winning over some of the finest families of Fifth Avenue, and the richest and best merchants of this city. His followers furnished him with plenty of money, carriages, a mansion in the city, and one in the country. Finally he was accused and detected of the worst crimes, and at last was sent to Sing Sing. While in jail he issued the following proclamation: "As I live, there shall be no more sowing in the earth until I, the twelfth and last of the apostles, am delivered out of the house of bondage." For fear of this proclamation many of the the farmers refused to sow, and they set to work to deliver him, and succeeded. He left the jail, and may be living yet to read what we now state to you.

It is really wonderful how easily men are deceived in religious matters. Let us study the Word, ask God's guidance in knowing and doing His will. Time is gone. I have said but little, much more might be said. In my next discourse I will introduce you to two old men who will visit Anti-Christ.

THE TWO WITNESSES.
Discourse XI.

Troublesome Times—Appearance of the Witnesses—Who are They?—How They can be Identified—Their Mission, Work, and Suffering—The Time and Circumstances of Christ's Coming.

"And I will give power unto My two witnesses, and they shall prophesy a thousand two hundred and three-score days, clothed in sackcloth."—Rev. ii. 3.

WE will all agree that the person and work of Anti-Christ are yet in the future. For while Anti-Christ is ruling in Jerusalem, and battling with the saints of the Most High, having conquered and plucked up by the roots three of the ten-horned kingdoms by his victories and cunning craft, and his alliance with the beast or the Church of Rome, he will become proud, blasphemous, and arrogant, and will at once try to force the people to worship the beast. He will claim to be the promised Jewish Messiah. He will enter the new Jewish Temple and actually sit enthroned as God incarnated, commanding the people to worship him. He will be so received by the Jews, some of the Israelites and the Romish Church, by the Communists and scientific infidels, and by "such as do wickedly against the covenant shall he corrupt by flatteries," men of understanding shall fall; indeed, Christianity will seem to be about destroyed.

Russia will aid by her influence his pretensions with a secret purpose to take the spoils and gain her long-desired object, Jerusalem and Palestine. England will stand aloof for a time, waiting an opportunity to interfere. Then will be a time to try men's faith—to test the Church. England and America will stand alone as representing freedom and religious liberty. "And then shall many be offended and shall betray one another, and shall hate one another. And many false prophets shall arise and deceive many; and because iniquity shall abound, the love of many shall wax cold; but he that shall endure unto the end shall be saved." This is the time when Communism, infidelity, and Romish Jesuitism will combine against God and liberty, and, thank heaven, this is the time appointed when they all will be destroyed. Then the kingdoms of this world will be given to the saints of the Most High. The struggle will be fierce, long, and terrible, but victory will be on the Lord's side.

In the very midst of these awful times there will appear two famous persons as witnesses for Jesus; one who will specially appear to the Jews, the other to Israel, and both testify for God and Jesus. These two witnesses will turn the tide of battle, confront Anti-Christ and his host, and give to the world new views of God and Providence.

These two old men, or witnesses, will be endowed with miraculous power to bring fire down from heaven, or turn the water streams into blood, and smite the earth with all manner of plagues, as often as they will. Their presence and power will cast a gloom o'er the nations of the earth, and Anti-Christ and his allies. They will finally be slain in the streets of Jerusalem. At the time of their death a great feast will be held to commemorate the victories of Anti-Christ and to inaugurate the setting up of an image of him in the temple. So in the city there will be peoples, kindreds, and tongues of many nations. And they will see the dead bodies of the two witnesses lying exposed and unburied in the streets for three days and a-half, for Anti-Christ will not suffer them to be buried. On the wings of the wind, by the telegraph and by signals, the news of their death will spread rapidly abroad to all the nations of the earth. Infidelity, and Communism, and the Jesuits will be emboldened. Feasting and rejoicing will be the order of the day. "And they that dwell upon the earth shall rejoice over them and make merry, and shall send gifts one to another, because these two prophets tormented them that dwelt upon the earth." That will be the merry wake for you—a wake that will suddenly end, and that, too, before the corpses are buried. The victories will be cut short and the rejoicing checked.

The spirit of life from God shall enter into the two exposed and corrupting bodies, and they shall stand upon their feet to defy Anti-Christ and his host, and laugh at the pains of death. Great fear will fall upon them who saw the dead so raised. This time the telegraphs will be muffled, and the news is kept back from the nations as much as possible; but astonishment ends not here, for over the destroying and now idolatrous city of Jerusalem hangs a peculiar cloud, and voices peal as thunder through the air, to call the attention of the multitudes. And when every eye is skyward, the cloud moves and opens, as a chariot of fire and glory, and rising in majesty and composure up above roofs, temples, and pinnacles, will be seen the two witnesses of Christ; they enter in and are borne heavenward. "And they ascended up to heaven in a cloud, and their enemies beheld them." Then, while the multitude are wrapt in wonder and all amazement, the pinnacles sway to and fro, the houses rock, the earth trembles, the walls of the city fall, and Olivet cleaves in twain. Then Anti-Christ is slain with many of his followers, and the remnant fear unto repentance. "And the same hour there was a great earthquake, and a tenth part of the city fell, and in the earthquake were slain of men seven thousand, and the remnant were affrighted, and gave glory to the God of heaven. And the seventh angel sounded, and there were great voices in heaven, saying, the kingdoms of this world are become the kingdoms of our Lord and of His Christ, and He shall reign for ever and ever.

These are some of the wonders yet to come. Then how say some that Anti-Christ has already been? The witnesses have not yet appeared; they have not yet wrought their miracles. The Lost Ten Tribes and the scattered Jews have not yet been gathered from all countries whither the Lord God hath scattered them, and placed in their own land, to go out no more, to be plucked up no more. Jerusalem is yet being trodden under foot, the land is comparatively desolate, no temple yet adorns the city, nor priest, nor Levite, attend at the altar. Pshaw! upon the Biblical interpreters of this day, who wilfully or ignorantly careen through the line of prophecies, despising the order established by God. They are like the girl with her novel, who cannot wait to read through the book, and take events in their order, but she turns to the last leaf to find the destiny of her hero. So men, born by passion and choice, skip by several of the prophecies, and harp everlastingly on the last— the coming of the blessed Jesus—" He whom the heavens must receive until the times of restitution of all things, which God hath spoken by the mouth of all His holy prophets since the world began " (Acts iii. 21). The world is not yet ready for Christ; it is yet too much upside down, too much confused. But God is in Christ reconciling the world unto Himself. It does not now look like God; so God and Christ, Providence and the Church, must work on till the house is in order for His return. "*Hon dei ouranon men dexasthai archri chronon apokataseos panton,*" whom, indeed, heaven must retain until the time of restoration of all things. If things are not now restored or reconciled, or in order, why, then, Christ cannot come. He will not come to put them in order; this He has left for and with the Church to do, and has promised to be with His Church to the end.

A few Sunday evenings ago, a brother kindly asked me Where the Church would be while Anti-Christ was reigning? I simply said anywhere and everywhere, wherever it happened to be. He thought the Church would be taken away by Christ; he referred me to several passages. I said, Come next Sunday evening, as those passages will be partly considered in my next sermon. He replied that he might be taken up by that time. All right, I said, then we will excuse you. Now, in the name of common sense, why have men, and why do men, down through the centuries, and now, entertain such views? Because every Bible reader must see that there are many prophecies that must be fulfilled before Christ can come—one of which is the appearance of the two witnesses of the text. They will be specially sent and commissioned to testify for Christ, as against Anti-Christ.

Let us now ascertain who these two witnesses are, or are to be. I find on examining the subject all manner of views set forth. And, as is often the case in studying a subject of this kind, I find few that agree—so much so, that at last I found relief in turning from what men said and thought to what God in His Holy Word had written and said.

First. They are two men. Second. They are sent to Jerusalem, which, because of the wickedness of the city at the time of their visit, will be called Sodom and Egypt; but, lest we should mistake the place from these names, John adds: "Where also our Lord was crucified." So Isaiah i. 10 says: "Hear the word of the Lord, ye rulers of Sodom; give ear unto the law of our God, ye people of Gomorrah." This fixes safely the place. Besides, the place is pointed out from the fact that they oppose Anti-Christ, who at that time we know will be at Jerusalem. Third. They are sent. You ask where they are sent from? The answer is, From heaven, from standing before the God of the whole earth. Fourth. Who sends them? We answer, Jesus—because the Book of the Revelation is "the Revelation of Jesus Christ, which God gave unto John." Fifth. What were they sent for? In the first place they were to be special witnesses for Jesus, for He calls them His two witnesses. In the second place, they were to prophesy, to be prophets in the fullest sense, to forecast the future, to interpret past and present; to work miracles; to assume control in directing State affairs. Sixth. It is worth your careful notice to note that they are not constituted witnesses by being sent; they are sent because they are witnesses. They are not then to be endowed with miraculous power; "these have power" in the present tense. These facts, if nicely considered, will at once suggest the persons.

Whoever they are, they must have gone from earth to heaven with their bodies, two persons who have escaped death, for their death takes place in Jerusalem. They must have been prophets before they left earth for heaven the first time. And in the third place, they must at some time and place have been special witnesses for Christ. In fact, they are two anointed ones, or, in other words, they are two persons who have been set apart and prepared for the very visit spoken of in the text.

Daniel, when speaking of them, and the visit spoken of in the text, calls one "the Ancient of Days;" the other one was "like the Son of Man." He represents these two persons as sitting in judgment on Anti-Christ, and the seven horns, or kingdoms. "And the ten horns that were in his head and of the other which came up, and before whom three fell; even of that horn that had eyes, and a mouth that spake very great things, whose look was more stout than his fellows (this is Anti-Christ). I beheld, and the same horn made war with the saints and prevailed against them, until the Ancient of Days came, and judgment was given to the saints of the Most High, and the time came that the saints possessed the kingdom" (Dan. vii. 20).

Many interpret "the Ancient of Days" and the "one like the Son of Man" to be Christ. They stagger not at the fact that there are two persons, and that they are introduced one to another, and that the Ancient of Days seems to be the greatest. It is nothing to such interpreters that there are two persons; these they make one. The one looking like the Son of Man they make out to be the Son of God, although Daniel says he only looked like Him. The judgment spoken of by Daniel they make out to be the general judgment, when, in fact, Daniel tells on what and where they sat in judgment—namely, at Jerusalem. About Anti-Christ—and that Anti-Christ is soon destroyed after this—and "as concerning the rest of the beasts (that is, the seven horns), they had their dominion taken away; yet their lives were prolonged for a season and a time." The vision and scene of the whole chapter belongs to this world, and the kingdom of the saints here spoken of is as much material and political as the other. The difference is, the rulers and people are Christians, they are called saints.

Every throne should be double-kinged; that is God's purpose, that is Heaven's plan. Christ wants no earthly throne excepting that way. As the Creator is Lord of lords and King of kings, so Christ after His resurrection assumed His Father's place, and stands to us as God to the Jews of old. All power was given to Him in heaven and in earth, therefore, He, Christ, has long since begun His reign, and He must continue to reign until He hath put all enemies under His feet. When David was king over Israel and Judah, so was God. We repeat, every throne should be double-kinged.

To this end will come these two witnesses. Who will they be? We answer, Moses and Elijah: these are the two brave old men now living and waiting to fulfil their mission. For hundreds of years they have been anointed. Moses is "the Ancient of Days;" the "one like the Son of man" is Elijah and Tishbite. This interpretation chimes in with the Divine Word, without twisting and distorting to make both ends meet.

We said these two were to be human: so they are. They being sent from heaven, we said they must have passed by death with their bodies; so they did. They were to be prophets; so they are, two of the grandest prophets of all. They were to have power over fire and water; so they had when they lived on earth. The bloody stream of the Nile gives witness for Moses. The parched land and time of drought speaks of Elijah in Ahab's time. They both called fire down on them who sought to hurt them. They were to be special witnesses of Christ; so they were on the Mount of Transfiguration. These two olive trees stood one on each side of the golden candlestick, Jesus; Peter, James, and John, testify to having seen Moses and Elijah. These two old veterans know Christ well, hence they will be sent to testify for Him against Anti-Christ. Moses is a Jew. He will appeal unto Jews, who will be found in the new temple, performing according to the old Mosaic law. He will change and lead his people from Anti-Christ to Christ. Elijah is an Israelite. He will specially bear testimony to the Israelite, his long-lost, but then restored brethren.

More in our next discourse on those two Christian heroes.

MOSES AND ELIJAH.

Discourse XII.

More About the Two Witnesses—Mormonism—God Ruling Among the Nations—Career of the Two Witnesses—Anti-Christ—The Throne and House of David.

"And the seventh angel sounded; and there were great voices in heaven, saying, The kingdoms of this world are become the kingdoms of our Lord, and of His Christ; and He shall reign for ever and ever."—Rev. ii. 15.

LAST Sabbath evening we called your attention to two special witnesses who are at a given time to appear at Jerusalem for a specific purpose. At the time of their appearance Anti-Christ will be reigning with great power and pomp. He will have succeeded in persuading the Jews and many others that he is the promised Jewish Messiah; this claim he will be able to sustain and confirm in the eyes of the multitude, from the very fact that he will, to all appearance, work miracles. Nor need we query that such a thing can take place. Look at some of the facts of our own day, and see how pliable human nature is. There are millions of people who sincerely believe that Leo XIII. is God's vicegerent, and that he is infallible. Take into account the Mormonism of this day, and see how terrible a thing in the name of Christianity can be established and maintained. Aye, in the nineteenth century, and in the United States of America. Or look in upon the Spiritualists and consider their claims and pretensions. Thousands upon thousands of them are persuaded that they are *en rapport* with heaven, and in communication with spirits and spirit-land. Then you will not be surprised at the pretensions, claims, and success of Anti-Christ. In our calm and unprejudiced consideration of these organisations, we are bound to admit that they have done more, and owe more for their success, to deception and error, than to truth and openness. Each in its turn has been caught in the act of deceiving, and has been frequently exposed, but of what avail? Truly but little. We do not mean that in these systems there is no good, for surely there is, but that the errors and deceptions are of so glaring a kind, that we wonder that anybody of common sense can be so easily led astray.

With these facts before us, can we wonder any longer that Anti-Christ shall be so successful? The very occasion and peculiar times and incidents of the reign of Anti-Christ will call for some special manifestations on the part of the Divine One that shall soberly and clearly confront the hollow and hypocritical pretensions of that age. Hence the appearance of the two witnesses—Moses the Ancient of Days, and Elijah the Tishbite, who will look like the Son of God.

Allow us to submit further evidence in proof that the two witnesses of John in Rev. xi. are none other than Moses and Elijah; for many passages of Holy Writ are sealed to the understanding till we comprehend who the two witnesses are, their mission and work. We will notice the attributive features of these witnesses as they are related by John in this chapter—that is, Rev. xi.

In the first place, there are two persons or individualities; this appears plainly from the tenor of the whole record. They are spoken of as "they, them, their mouth, their feet, as dying and being resurrected." But, strange to say, after all this plainness of speech, men have become so accustomed to spiritualise and generalise that Anti-Christ stood for Rome, and naturally enough, have generalised Anti-Christ, they must do the same with the two witnesses; hence they found them in the Churches of the Waldenses and Albigenses. In such an interpretation nearly all the attributive features of these witnesses are ignored. Such as that they had power to work miracles, to lie unburied in the streets of Jerusalem for three days and a half. Some have laboured to prove that the Old and New Testaments were these witnesses, others that they were symbolised by the law and gospel. Again, some that the two sacraments, baptism and the Lord's Supper, were these two witnesses, and so on, almost without end. These instances will suffice for our present purpose; for surely any of you reading God's own Word need not so blunder.

In the second place, Jesus calls them His two witnesses. Now, in what sense were they His? for such they are now. Not that they will be His when they appear, but they will appear to oppose Anti-Christ at Jerusalem because they are sent. The prophets are all witnesses; for, as Peter says, "To Him gave all the prophets witness." The apostles were witnesses, and all believers are witnesses for Jesus; yet these two are so in a special and pre-eminent sense. Let any one read the account of the transfiguration of Jesus, and the circumstances attendant thereon, and all will be plain. Moses and Elias (another spelling for Elijah) we find were present, as well as Peter, James, and John. When Christ was transfigured, "Behold, there appeared unto them Moses and Elias" (Matt. xvii. 3.) These two persons talked with Jesus, "and spake of His decease which he should accomplish at Jerusalem." Thus, then, they were special witnesses for Christ, and so they will come again and witness for Him in the time appointed.

The number of days we must take in a literal sense; here the 1260 days and 3½ days are the days appointed for their work and death. It is well to remember that many of the prophetic numbers contain a double prophecy. Thus 1,260 here may be coincident with the treading down of Jerusalem by Mahommedanism. But whether it is or not, does not vitiate the literal quantity when applied to these two witnesses. In the third place, they are called two olive trees and two candlesticks standing before the God of the whole earth. The figurative meaning will be found by finding some passages where two trees are mentioned in the interpretation given—such a passage by Zechariah iv. Here the prophet saw two olive trees and asked of the angel the meaning; and the angel said, "Knowest thou not what these be?" And I said, "No, my Lord." Then said he, "*These are two anointed ones that stand by the Lord of the whole earth.*" The simple meaning is, that the two olive trees mean two persons; who are in heaven at present, but are anointed—that is, set apart, selected for some distinct work for God.

Moses and Elijah evidently were anointed and specially selected, for it is probable they both escaped death. The wonder connected with the disappearance of Moses and the translation of Elijah now finds some measure of explanation. None doubt the translation of Elijah. John the Baptist was not Elias, except he was to go before Christ in the spirit and power of Elias; in this sense John stood for Elias. John the Baptist prepared the way of Christ the first time, so will Elias for Christ's second coming. The record of Moses's departure from this world is as mysterious as it is dramatic. But, certainly, neither the mysterious nor the dramatic have any meaning excepting we allow something Divinely special. To die as other people, would mean nothing on the line of specialities; but he did not so die. He went from the people alive, no one saw him die or dead. He went up into Mount Horeb and never returned. So, so far as the people were concerned, he was to them a dead man, for he went from them no more to return. The word death in Hebrew has not less than six meanings, one of which is simply to disappear. This is the meaning that we must attach to the death of Moses. Neither his grave or body have ever been found.

There is a peculiar passage in the book of Jude where "Michael the archangel, when contending with the devil, he disputed about the body of Moses, durst not bring against him a railing accusation, but said, The Lord rebuke thee." Now Satan then had power over death in some way Divinely permitted. Paul says (Heb. ii. 14), speaking of Christ, "Forasmuch then as the children are partakers of flesh and blood, He also Himself likewise took part of the same; that through death He might destroy him *that had the power of death*—that is, the devil." When God was translating Moses, passing him by death, Satan fought with Michael, who was God's messenger, to inflict the sting of death on Moses, and although Michael carried Moses on by death into the presence of God, Satan durst not bring a railing accusation against him.

Jude, in his epistle, probably quoted from one of the now lost books of Revelation, which was entitled, "The Ascension or Assumption of Moses the Servant of God." The Church father, Origen, makes mention of this work; but, like the book and prophecies of Enoch, from which Jude makes a quotation, it has been lost, they having served their purpose. The fairest and most generous interpretation, then, is, that Moses did not die the ordinary death, but disappeared, was, in fact, translated, anointed, and set apart for a special work in connection with his own people, the Jews, in the days of the coming Anti-Christ. Thus, without any trouble, he could appear with Elijah on the Mount of Transfiguration. And it is worthy of note that before he disappeared in Horeb—the sacred writer is mindful to tell us " Moses was an hundred and twenty years old when he died—*his eye was not dim nor his natural force abated*" (Deut. xxiv. 7). But, supposing Moses died naturally, there is nothing unreasonable or irregular in concluding that God resurrected him as a mortal for future use. True, he will die again as a witness; so there are in heaven now eight persons who have died twice in this world—namely:—

The child raised by Elijah (1 Kings xvii. 21).

The child of Elisha (2 Kings iv. 35).

The Moabite soldier who came to life on touching the bones of Elisha (2 Kings xiii. 21).

The daughter of Jairus (Luke viii. 55).

The widow's son at Nain (Luke vii. 15).

Lazarus of Bethany (John xi. 44).

Dorcas or Tabitha by Peter (Acts ix. 40).

Eutychus by Paul (Acts xx. 10).

Anti-Christ will be a great electrician; electricity by that time will be a fearful power in the hands of science. Edison with his genius and marvellous discoveries, and others of like gifts, will have perfected the use of this agent in a wonderful degree. Anti-Christ will make use of this power to cower his enemies and bring them in fear-subjection. He will bring fire down from heaven. The two witnesses, however, will be clothed with divine power; they will be able to bring fire by a simple command—this they both understand and used when on earth.

Moses called fire down upon the 250 rebellious Korahthites, as we read in Numbers xvi. Ahab, the King of Israel, thought to punished and compel the obedience of Elijah; but God gave fire from heaven in answer to the prophet's prayer. So when Ahaziah sent a captain and fifty men to bring Elijah into the king's presence, they found him sitting on the top of a hill and commanded him to come down. "And Elijah answered and said to the captain of fifty, If I be a man of God, then let fire come down from heaven, and consume thee and thy fifty. And there came down fire from heaven, and comsumed him and his fifty" (2 Kings i. 10). Thus will these two anointed ones be able to contend with Anti-Christ and all the powers of scientific infidels. "If any man hurt these two witnesses, by the very means used so shall they be killed."

"These have power to shut heaven, that it rain not in the days of their prophecy, and have power over waters to turn them to blood." To whom would these gifts and attributes apply better than to Elijah, who in the days of the wicked King Ahab sealed the heavens against rain for three years and a half? and to Moses, who, when contending with Pharaoh, turned the sweet flowing Nile into a stream of blood? What two prophets had such a wide range of prophetic energy and liberty as Moses and Elijah? None. Well may the Revelator say, then, of them, that they can smite the earth with all manner of plagues as often as they will.

By awful and sublime manifestations the world shall see that God rules in the heaven and on the earth. They shall learn that Anti-Christ is a false Christ. Then shall fear and repentance fall upon the people. The Jews shall be convinced, and converted, and persuaded by the appearance of their beloved Moses. They shall know of a truth that the Messiah has been, and is waiting to come again. Referring to that time the prophet Zechariah calls it a time of trembling, the time of a terrible siege. But he tells us that "The Lord also shall save the tents of Judah first, that the glory of the House of David, and the glory of the inhabitants of Jerusalem, do not magnify themselves against Judah." Thus we learn that the Jews, who have been so long despised and bereft of a king, country, and government, shall see through the great mystery of Providence first. The House of David is found in the royal family of England. The Jews, seeing this, will invite, in concert with all the inhabitants of Jerusalem, the English Government to take charge of their affairs.

"Then shall the children of Judah and the children of Israel be gathered together and appoint themselves one *head*" (Hosea i. 2). The Jews will then be Christians. "For they shall look upon Him whom they have pierced; and they shall mourn for Him, as one mourneth for his only son."

At this time the whole world will be amazed and confounded at the destruction of Anti-Christ and his host. The Jews, the House of David, and the Lost Tribes, Israel, the Saxons, will hold a council in Jerusalem. David's house, which God selected, and throne, both of which the Almighty promised perpetuity to, shall be found and recognised in the English throne and royal family. The Saxon race shall distinctively appear as long-lost Israel. So that the Jews, and David's House, and Israel, will unite and acknowledge Christ as Lord and Master. They will make known to America, who stands for Manasseh, and all the colonies, the decision of the said council; all parties will see, and accept, and federate for the world's conquest and peace.

This federation of the ancient people, the literal seed of Abraham, will cause jealousies and alliances on the part of the rest of the world, excepting some portions of France, Austria, and Prussia. The beast, dragon, and Anti-Christ's force, that will survive the shock of the two witnesses, will all unite for an onslaught upon England, but especially Palestine. Russia, though nominally Christian, will join the beast or Romish

Church. The dragon means the Pagan portion of the world. Thus will be inaugurated the battle of Armageddon, the issues of which we are permitted to know through Revelation. Then will the kingdoms of this world become the kingdoms of our Lord and His Christ.

With many, and to many, these things are but dreams; they are chimerical. But one thing is certain: the history of the Church and Providence in the future are appallingly grand. Providence was grand in leading forth His people of old from Egypt. But He will be no less grand when He shall set His hand a second time to recover His people, as He has promised to do.

"Behold, the days come, saith the Lord, that I will raise unto David a righteous branch, and a king shall reign and prosper, and shall execute judgment and justice in the earth. In His days Judah shall be saved, and Israel shall dwell safely, and this is His name whereby He shall be called, the Lord our Righteousness." (That is, the ruler of God's choice—a king, then, in fact, by divine right.) "Therefore, behold, the days come, saith the Lord, that they shall no more say, The Lord liveth, which brought up the children of Israel out of the land of Egypt; but, The Lord liveth, which brought up and which led the seed of the House of Israel out of the North country, and from all countries whither I had driven them, and they shall dwell in their own land" (Jer. xxiii. 68).

God has now one of the seed of David on the throne, and He has had a Jew doing her bidding, executing her decrees over and for Israel. For though Israel were to be numerous and powerful, yet to David's seed belongs the throne.

The recent Congress was but a forerunner of the one yet to come. The crownless king, Disraeli, who forced the Congress, was, perhaps, an unconscious instrument in the hands of Providence. But whether he was or not, he has hastened on the day with lightning speed. Forth from the recent Congress he went, having once again linked the destinies of England to the Continent, which had been so strangely severed, till Russia, Italy, Austria, France, and Spain might each test the other, and each find their appointed place. Now, again, England pledges herself a continental power—nay, more—an Asiatic Power. She came forth from the Congress the virtual ruler of Turkey, the owner of Palestine.

BATTLE OF ARMAGEDDON.
Discourse XIII.

The Combatants on Both Sides—Who the "Kings of the East" are—The Great Napoleonic Idea—Disraeli, Lincoln, and Grant—England's Policy in Turkey—Future Wars and Intrigues—The Great Battle-field—Gathering of the Nations—Earthquakes—Jerusalem a Seaport.

"And He gathered them together into a place called in the Hebrew tongue Armageddon."—Rev. xvi. 16.

CHRISTIAN students and prophetic writers are generally agreed on three things touching this great event. First, that there is to be such a decisive battle fought. Second, that it will take place in some part of Palestine. Third, that this great struggle will be final, the end of war, the beginning of the Millennium morn.

In the Scriptures the contestants are pointed out, as they rally under the standards of the *dragon*, the beast, and *Anti-Christ*, on one side, and on the other, under the standard of David, will be the *called*, the *chosen*, and the *faithful*; or, in other words, the Ten Lost Tribes as found chiefly in the Saxon race, with all who sincerely believe on the Lord Jesus Christ.

In another sermon we pointed out to you the plain fact of the existence of David's throne and David's seed as found and seen specially in the throne of England. We there see how faithfully God has kept His promise to David and His people. For God frequently told David that his throne should be established unto all generations, and of David's seed there should never be wanting a man to sit thereon. It is the permanence, the grandeur, and progressive character of this throne and people that make it a fitting type of Christ and His Church. Nay, more, it is on this throne that Christ now sits, so far as this world goes; and it is through this people that He reigns, and He will and must reign until He has conquered a universal peace. It is a delusion too long entertained by the Church to think that David's throne and seed have not now, nor for centuries had, an existence. It is a delusion that we should not entertain for a moment, to think that the Ten Tribes of Israel are lost for ever, or that their work or mission is fulfilled. As surely as the Two Tribes, Judah and Levi, now exist, fulfilling and filling in the outlines of prophetic history, so surely are Reuben, Simeon, Zebulon, Issachar, Dan, Gad, Asher, Naphtali, Benjamin, Ephraim, and Manasseh in existence, answering the purpose of an all-seeing Providence.

Who are the kings of the East spoken of in the Scriptures? We answer, They are the royal ones of the House of David. The word king, both in Hebrew and Greek, mean such. This seed God chose, and made them royal by that very selection. They have been away from their own land, Palestine, wandering and dwelling in the West. But God in Providence is preparing a way for their return. In connection with the pouring out of the sixth vial upon the great river of the Euphrates, or upon Turkey, as most writers agree, the waters are to dry up—that is, Turkey is to decay, to be absorbed. And why? "That the way of the kings of the East might be prepared" (Rev. xvi. 12).

These kings have been away from the East, and their return is assured, and the preparation for such return is to be seen at this time, and in connection with the decay of Turkey. If Turkey, as symbolised by the river Euphrates, is drying up, then these kings must be advancing Eastwards; and so they are.

The crownless king, Disraeli, who, like many other men God has raised up, was for these times an index finger pointing out the way of Providence. He was a receptive agent of Divine force, to the intent that he interpreted a Divine purpose. He may have known, or he may not, that he was so directed of heaven. The prophets of old were seldom permitted to interpret or understand their own prophecies. If they asked, like Daniel, the meaning, they were told to "go their way," for oftentimes the words were "closed up and sealed until the time of the end." No wonder this man, against all England nearly, and to the amazement of all the world, proclaimed the Queen of England the Empress of India, for the way of the kings of the East must be prepared.

Napoleon Bonaparte's grand idea was to prepare the way of the kings of the East, and make himself and his descendants these kings. "Conquer England and the world is ours," he said. But when his secret and well-prepared assault on England was revealed and frustrated by a chain of providential events, he hit upon another plan to get possession of Palestine. Seventy years ago he invited all the leading Jews of the world to a secret council in Paris; he wished them to aid him in getting possession of Palestine. He pretended to want their return. He gave them certain privileges and laboured to procure more from the other nations; he did much for the Jews in enlarging their liberties and taking away from them the curse of society. The one idea that is distinctly Napoleonic, is to possess Palestine. The late Napoleon had his idea, and in his day this idea had become a part of France; so much so, that France thought herself to be then and now the real protector of Palestine. It was for this idea that she allied with England and Turkey in the Crimean war. It was to keep Russia back from possessing the holy places. Not till France was weakened could England advance on her way East rapidly; so Germany was used to destroy her prestige and cause her to stand aside till England proceeds on her way homeward.

It was a comely sight, some few years ago, to see two Jews closeted together making a secret bargain—one had power, the other had money. The man of power asked the man of money to lend him twenty million dollars; it was done. At once the man of power purchases with this twenty millions part of his fatherland back again—the Suez Canal. This very canal is on the boundary of the land of Palestine as given to Abraham centuries ago. By this very route the old patriarch entered the Promised Land. It was fitting, indeed, that this should be the first piece purchased back. No one knew save those directly interested. England murmured and France protested, but the thing was done. Poor France, bleeding and divided, could do but little; for Disraeli and Rothschild had done the work. The way of the kings of the East must be prepared. So on they go. A man who executes a Divine purpose is always strong. Abraham Lincoln, in the history of America, was so chosen and led of God. The politicians, and statesmen, and generals, and many of the people were against him at first; but the Lord was with him, so he marched on to victory, the country following in the wake. And though dead, not forgotten, the country and the civilised world are marching on after him, and now they have nearly overtaken him. Lincoln's ideas and the country's are nearly equal. A man led of God is generally a good distance behind, and the people led by such a man are equally as far behind him as he is behind God. But this nation and Abraham Lincoln are now one, and in those things in which they once were divided they are a unit, with more than the honoured Lincoln; for they are a unit with God and providence. Thus follows the English nation in the wake of Disraeli, and the world is coming on behind, and the day will come when all will be a unit. It does not shock our idea of human honesty much when we learn that this crownless king played a double game with Russia and Turkey. It was intensely Jewish, but if it were only Jewish, then it would be very detestable; it was more, it was divine in part. " Had the princes of this world known, they would not have crucified the Prince of Glory." Had the princes of the late Berlin Congress known the double game being played by one of the quietest of their number, they would not have done as they did. Turkey in Asia was given over to England's protection; aye, yes, that included Palestine. The island of Cyprus was given over entirely—surely the way of the kings of the East is being grandly prepared.

Why did not the Congress hand over to England's protection Turkey in Europe? For reasons good and sufficient. Turkey in Europe will be the cause of much strife, of several wars, and of strange alliances; hence it would not have done for Israel-England to be mixed up with it. Constantinople alone, of European Turkey, England will keep. Israel is to be much preserved from war, until the great battle of Armageddon comes on. Against that time she will have to husband her strength and resources. It is marvellous now to think that what the Congress settled as belonging to England, none disputed—all was peace. But Russia's share and Austria's were in arms. Servia, Greece, Roumania, and all the Turkish provinces rebelled and were in a state of disquietude, that portends war and strife again in a few years. But England will have nothing to do with it, excepting that Russia and Austria, with the consent of Germany, Italy, and France, are to set a precedent for England, which in a few years she will need. It is plain that if Russia and Austria can force by arms the conditions of the Berlin Congress, England will be at liberty to do the same without any interference even from France. The Congress handed over to England's keeping Turkey. England, then, can make Turkey do her bidding by force of arms sustained by the very precedent already set. Thus will Israel-England open up Palestine for Christian settlement. The Mahommedans will murmur and resist to have the holy places taken from them, but no matter; England, when the time comes, will enforce it. It is just here that Turkey and England will dispute, and in each dispute England will find a reason for drawing the lines a little tighter around poor Turkey.

The contestants on one side at the great battle of Armageddon, you remember, are the dragon, the beast, and Anti-Christ. Now what people is represented by the term dragon? We answer, the Pagan nations and authorities, just as the Chinese have on their standards to-day a dragon, as we have the eagle. The Mahommedans, Hindoos, Brahmins, Buddhists, and all Pagan idolators, are summed up in the word dragon. At present, England is tolerant with the subjects and adherents of these different worshippers and religions; but the time will come when she will no longer tolerate the same; thus will they arraign themselves against her in the battle of Armageddon. This will come to pass as the gradual destruction of Mormonism in our country. This system has been fortified by law; now laws are being arraigned against it. It is now only tolerated, and in a short time it will be wiped out of existence.

The final battle referred to in the text is to occur at a place called in the Hebrew tongue Armageddon, the literal meaning of which is at the mount of Megido. In olden times there was a city called Megiddon; it stood in what is now called the great plain of Esdraelon—a plain that lies midway between the Sea of Galilee and the Mediterranean. It was also called Jezreel. The prophet Hosea speaks of this place, battle, and time all by this one word. Referring to the time when the children of Judah and of Israel are gathered together under one head in their own land, he says, "For great shall be the day of Jezreel" (Hos. i. 11). It is spoken of in the Scriptures and history as the valley of Jehoshaphat, because here Jehoshaphat, the King of Judah, gained a great victory; for here the Lord fought against the enemies of Israel, as He will in the coming battle. Joel iii. 12 says, referring to this coming struggle, "Let the heathen be waked up and come to the valley of Jehoshaphat; for there will I sit to judge all the heathen round about."

There is one name given to this time and battle that is very significant and striking. Have you ever noticed it? If not, let me call your attention to it. It is called "That great day of God Almighty," by John in the chapter of the text. The day of the Lord of hosts by Isaiah. Ezek. xxx. 3: "Howl ye! Woe worth the day! For the day of the Lord is near: it shall be the time of the heathen." And Joel says, "Multitudes, multitudes, in the valley of decision; for the day of the Lord is near in the valley of decision. By the prophets Amos, Obadiah, Zephaniah, Zechariah, Malachi, and apostles Paul and Peter, it is called the day of the Lord.

You ask if this battle may not have taken place. We answer, No. Of such a battle we have no record. Again, it will be the end of the war—the final overthrow of Paganism, the beast, and Anti-Christ. Malachi says, "Behold I will send you the prophet Elijah before the coming of that great and dreadful day of the Lord." Elijah has not yet been a witness. At the time of this great battle nature is to take a wonderful part. As when Christ was on the cross, the sun darkened, the rocks rent, the mountains shook, so in connection with this battle there shall be some strange wonders—earthquakes, thundering, lightning, hail, and fire. The Mount of Olives will divide; the valley of the Dead Sea will fill with water and join to the Mediterranean; Jerusalem will become a seaport; an appointed centre from which, being central to all the world, will go forth the ships of the Lord. The city of Jerusalem, between this time and that, will be considerably enlarged, then it will divide into three parts. At the time of this dividing John says, "That the cities of the nations are to fall"—London, Paris, Berlin, Rome, St. Petersburg, and many others—that all may turn to Jerusalem, the capital appointed of heaven.

If you wish to know more of the particulars of this day, read the prophets, study what John the Revelator says under the sixth vial and sixth seal. With awful grandeur and with terrible majesty have the sacred writers set forth this day and time.

That this day will come, who will deny? Look at the world ripening for this day. Here, in our own land, as well as others, the forces are maturing, the agents are at work. Many of the events of the past year we were permitted to forecast by looking into the future through the prophets, and onward yet we look. And the events coming are neither less in number, merit, or force, than those passed. Keep the events of prophecy in their proper order lest they confuse you. The Jews and Ten Lost Tribes are to be found and possess Palestine before this battle. Anti-Christ is to appear. The two witnesses, Moses and Elijah, are to appear. And Jesus, our beloved Master, will not come till the world is settled long in perpetual peace—till the house is prepared for the bride, then shall He come. But with lightning speed events are crowding on along the ages. The accumulative forces of centuries are pressing hard upon time present. The time of the end is near—not the end of time, but the time appointed of God in which certain great things are to be accomplished. Eighteen hundred years ago John cried out, "Loose the four angels which are bound in the great river Euphrates. And the four angels were loosed, which were prepared for an hour, and a day, and a month, and a year" (Rev. ix. 14).

The Turkish Power originated on the banks of the Euphrates.

It was first divided into four Sultanies—namely, Bagdad, Aleppo, Damascus, and Cesarea. These are typified under four angels. Their time was to be 396 years and a fraction—an hour, day, month, and year. Thus, taking a day for a year, 365 for the year, thirty for the month, one for the day, and we have 396. So from the taking of Bagdad by the Turks in 1057, which was the overthrow of the Saracens, until the capture of Constantinople in 1453, which overthrew the Greek Empire, we have just 396 years. And the time for the drying up of Turkey is at hand; and so it comes to pass.

Dear friends, how wonderful are the dealings of our God! Can we shut our eyes to His divine revelation? Let us be wise in the day of grace, taking heed to the sure Word of prophecy, as unto a light that shineth in a dark place. The world indeed is dark, and all confusion. But His Word shews unto us order in all this confusion, blessed be His name. More next Sunday evening.

ARMAGEDDON AND THE PYRAMID.

Discourse XIV.

The Forces in the Battle—Time of its Occurrence—Mistakes of Adventists—A Church "Strike" Wanted—The Hard Times after 1882—History of the World till 1933—Hine's Theory.

"These shall make war with the Lamb, and the Lamb shall overcome them; for He is Lord of lords and King of kings; and they that are with Him are called, and chosen, and faithful."—Rev. xviii. 14.

LAST Sunday evening we considered the subject of the great battle of Armageddon. This evening we will take up the same subject for further consideration. This battle, we learn, is to be very terrible, such a one as the world has not had. Fearful as some of the wars of the past have been, this will overshadow them all in skill, fierceness, number, slaughter, devastation, and wide-spread ruin. It will, in some respects, be like one of the wars of olden times. For in this struggle God is again to take a direct part, as He did for His people Israel and Judah in times of old. Again shall the forces of nature do battle for God and His people; again they shall be full of instinctive revenge. Hear us, and believe us, Dennis Kearney, Providence will then "pool the issues" of the *called*, the *chosen* and the *faithful*. The called are the Jews, the chosen are Israelites, and the faithful embrace all of every nation who believe in Christ. Then many will wade in pools of blood and perish, The birds of prey are to hold high carnival on the dead bodies of the slain, The spirit of Satan, that now worketh in the children of disobedience, will pool the issues of hell and death in the hosts of the *dragon, beast,* and *false prophet.* For though these three powers are diverse in their aims, professions, and intents, yet we learn from many passages of the Divine Book that they will join hands and agree upon a common policy, federating together that they may contend with the called, the chosen, and the faithful. "And I saw three unclean spirits like frogs come out of the mouth of the dragon, and out of the mouth of the beast, and out of the mouth of the false prophet. For they are the spirits of devils working miracles, which go forth unto the kings of the earth and of the whole world, to gather them to the battle of that great day of God Almighty" (Rev. xvi. 13, 14). Here indeed will be a pooling of the issues, a pooling that will divide the whole world into two forces or parties.

Now the canvass has begun, preparations are going on, party lines are being drawn, powers are concentrating, and men are rallying under their respective standards, getting the world ripe and ready for the coming generations, into whose hands the destinies of that day will be cast. Few of us now living can personally take part in that final battle, excepting as we do so by impressing the unborn millions with our ideas. Like as David prepared the material for the building of the temple, and his son Solomon carried forward the same, so the work of this generation is simply preparatory, and that of the coming will be executive.

Several wars will take place before that of Armageddon, which in their nature will be fierce and terrible. Still these will all be preparatory—leading on to the day of decision and the battle final. On this point many err, and their error has a pernicious influence on the Church and the world. They interpret the preparatory signs as if they were final; hence the end with such is too near. A sincere anxiety takes possession of their soul, which utterly unfits them to judge aright the signs of the times and tokens of providence. Thus were a portion of the Advent Church thrown into confusion the 8th of last July because they had fixed upon the seventh as the time for the ending of the world. And human folly and haste will repeat itself again on the 10th of April next, because another portion of the Advent brethren have fixed upon the 9th of April as the time of the end. It is a wonder the first did not take the 4th of July instead of the seventh, for then a stranger might think the end was nigh in some of our cities; or why didn't the other party select the first of April, for no doubt it would have proved a more propitious day? But thus it is, and will be again before the appointed time of Heaven comes. Man is a creature of haste and sudden impulse, especially so in his religious experience. Kings and nations, Churches and sects, have laboured hard in times past to force the issues of Providence and give speed and certainty to times and events.

The prophecies affecting our days are clear; so much so, that he who runs may read, if need be. But an impatient activity urges men on, bedazzling their eyes, which at once unnerves and unfits them for reading or judging. "In your patience possess ye your souls," said the blessed Master to His disciples of old, and not less through them unto us.

"Order is Heaven's first law," it has been said; and surely order pervades the prophecies. But the pulpits in general over-ride this order, and are not slow to malign such men as Edward Hine, of London, England, when the fact is, that his theory of the prophecies and mode of interpretation are vastly more natural, responsive, and reasonable than the ill-adjusted, unnatural, and non-responsive, system of current theology. A person is under obligation to use that key for the unlocking of prophecy which fits the best, and that responds to providential events the most natural, without regard to the antiquated systems and mode of Church, sect, or college theology. Hine's theory, as it is called sometimes, is as much superior to the old system of interpretation as the railway Pullman car is to the ricketty old stage coach.

The Anglo-Saxon Israel theory neither destroys or introduces any new principle, but discovers and applies that which had been long hidden. The introduction of steam and electricity did not destroy or produce any new principle, but simply discovered and applied, in an improved form, that which had been in the world from Adam down till now.

As men in science, mechanics, and practical life, throw overboard men and things of the past, so should we in theology, Church life and experience, when we can do better. Reverence for persons, and respect for ideas, should not enslave us. Let us move on, doing better and better. We do not care to believe all the theology of a Martin Luther. When we can make an advance on men or theories we should do so. Bacon and Newton are now in part rejected, without intending, or in fact doing them any dishonour or disrespect. So are Calvin and Wesley, on the same principle, by every good theologian. If a theory be advanced that opens up the Scriptures, and especially the prophecies, better than those before existing, let the pulpit accept it, throwing aside its mawkishness and age-entrenched stupidity. I have no hesitation to say, after over twenty-five years' experience with preachers and pulpits, that the majority of preachers are lazy and indifferent in study. For this reason many of them are deterred from examining any new theory. Many have said to me, and written to me, that if they accepted the Lost Tribe theory it would destroy nearly all their old sermons, and necessitate the making of new ones—a work they were not willing to undertake. It will, therefore, be a long time before the pulpit is reformed. In these days there are many strikes. While in Canada, on my vacation, I agreed to lecture for a Church choir on the prophet Jeremiah's visit to Ireland. But some preachers banded together and stopped it; and, in consequence of it, the choir struck and refused to sing the following Sunday. Passing by this strike, I really wish the laymen would strike and call the pulpit to an account and rouse it from its lethargy, and demand that it should untrammel itself and be free and equal to the age and demand. I have met with miserly persons who didn't believe in beautiful churches, or the missionary cause, or any cause indeed that wanted money.

They would argue for plainness, and so on. The secret of their peculiar ideas on these matters was to be found in there stinginess and their love of money. They advocated such theories because it saved them from contributing. Like a man I met with on my vacation tour who said he had saved forty dollars a year by pretending to be angry with the minister or some of the deacons when they came round collecting money. Some ministers, no doubt the majority of them, talk about holding on to the old landmarks, and being orthodox for the very reason that to make a move implies labour, which they are not willing to give, hence they prate about orthodoxy and landmarks as a pretext to cover over their indifference. He is the most orthodox who searches after the truth and keeps up with the age. "Prove all things, hold fast that which is good," says Paul. These pretended followers of Paul say: "Prove nothing, hold fast what you have got."

It is as plain as A, B, C, that the Bible teaches the return of the Jews and Ten Lost Tribes of Israel to the land of Palestine. Also, that after they have settled in this land Anti-Christ appears. The dragon and beast are already in existence but Anti-Christ is not; but the spirit of Anti-Christ is. When Israel and Judah are settled and prosperous in the old fatherland, then is to come on the battle of Armageddon. Thank Heaven! that though the struggle will be awful, it will be final, and victory will turn on the Lord's side. Then will be set up a kingdom that shall endure in abiding peace and prosperity for at least a thousand years. The world will nestle in regaling plenty and great assurance. This kingdom is to be set up in the latter days of the four kingdoms spoken of by Daniel. By this we understand that these kingdoms will have their day, and by succession, after a time, run out. These kingdoms—namely, Babylon, Persia, Greece, and Rome— are now disappearing. Rome, politically, is gone, Persia will soon be absorbed, also Greece. Babylon, being continued in the Empire of Russia, has yet a glorious future before it for the next fifty years or so, then she will disappear to rise no more. The cry will go forth, "Babylon is fallen." In Nebuchadnezzar's image you will remember that the stone cut out of the mountain began to destroy the metallic image upward, hence these kingdoms will disappear in reverse order to their origin. First Rome, which has gone; next Greece, which has nearly gone; then Persia, and then Russia. The new kingdom will fill the world. Already it foreshadows the outlines of possession by its immense territory of to-day. Then a scion of the House of David shall be enthroned in Jerusalem. All the other great capitals will have been destroyed. It is surprisingly grand to read of that day, king, and kingdom. Let me read to you a few verses from Jeremiah, chap. xxiii. "Behold, the days come, saith the Lord, that I will raise unto David a righteous branch, and a King shall reign and prosper, and shall execute judgment and justice in the earth. In His days Judah shall be saved, and Israel shall dwell safely; and this is His name whereby He shall be called; the Lord our Righteousness. Therefore, behold, the days come, saith the Lord, that they shall no more say, The Lord liveth, which brought up the children of Israel out of the land of Egypt; but, The Lord liveth, which brought up and which led the seed of the House of Israel out of the North country, and from all countries whither I had driven them; and they shall dwell in their own land." The words, "that day," are often used, and if we desire to know when that day is, we have data in the great fact that it is the other side of Armageddon, and Armageddon is the other side of the settlement of Israel and Judah in Palestine.

I wish, just here, to correct many of you, as well as some of the public journals. Of late I have frequently seen it stated in the papers that I predicted the end of the world in 1882. And many persons have actually asked if I did really think so. The truth of the matter is, in my sermons on the Great Pyramid

I pointed out to you the remarkable fact that the Grand Gallery was 1,882 inches long. Beginning with the birth of the Saviour, these inches stand for years. This Gallery suddenly ends, excepting that it is continued in a narrow passage, the narrowest in the whole building, for fifty-three inches. Then comes the King's Chamber, which before you enter, you pass under a portcullis in the form of an olive leaf. In this chamber all is equal, quiet, and central. Now, what I think this pillar of witness in Egypt teaches (see Isa. xix. 19) is, that about the year 1882 the world will enter upon a time of great trouble, war, anarchy, and famine, and for fifty-three years these troubles will continue more or less. Then about 1935 will occur the battle of Armageddon, which will be the finishing touch, the end of war. I arrive at this, when I follow the teachings of the Pyramid, by adding 1882 and 53, which gives me 1935. Even then the world will not end, but only begin the millennium morn, which will last for a thousand years or more.

Now corresponding to these facts are the events of Providence. As when Spring is nigh we know by certain signs, so we know from the Scriptures, Providence, and Pyramidal teaching, where we stand and the season we are in. " O ye hypocrites, ye can discern the face of the sky, but can ye not discern the signs of the times?" said Jesus to the proud and critical Pharisees and learned and doubting Sadducees. These parties affected to be specially wise and discriminating in their knowledge of the times and seasons, and interpreting the prophets and writings of Moses. Yet their conduct betrayed their ignorance, for they saw not the end of that grand old prophetic age, nor the fading symbolism of the temple, nor the departing glory and decay of their nation. They knew not the fulness of the time in which they lived, though it bulged out like a mountain. They did not know that *one time hath ended,* another *time begun* for they still dated their documents 4032 of the world, when it, was the year of our Lord and their Lord 32.

The antediluvians stand condemned because they were willingly ignorant of the Providential tokens and signs of the times. They set at nought the teachings and warnings of Noah, and in exulting pride they rejected the idea of a special Providence. Their faith, like many in this day, was planted and nourished by the laws of nature, and the analogous continuance of the same, not accepting the doctrine of a Divine Providence. They cried aloud, "Where is the promise of His coming? For since the fathers fell asleep, all things continue as they were from the beginning of the creation."

Do you, like the Jews of old, demand more signs, when those given you are not understood, or, if understood, they are undervalued? The prophets have been lavish in portraying the calamities of the *last days*, or the times into which we are entering. For the words *last days* are the few years preceding the battle of Armageddon. The calamities of these days are of four kinds: First, social disorders; second, religious feuds and wars; third, wonderful political disturbances; fourth, temporal or physical disasters. Of the social condition of these last days, Paul instructs us: "This know, also, that in the last days perilous times shall come." Then he groups together nineteen immoral attributes of the social state of these last days: "Men shall be lovers of their own selves, covetous, boasters, proud blasphemers, disobedient (to parents especially), unthankful, unholy, without natural affection, truce breakers, false accusers, incontinent, fierce despisers, traitors, heady, highminded, lovers of pleasure more than God, formal in religion" (2 Tim. iii.). What, we ask, will be the state of society when the social condition becomes such?

The religious feuds and persecutions of the last days we can but faintly conceive. It was terrible when the beast, two hundred years ago, held sway. The Inquisition, the rack, the stake, and all the horrors of a wise age will be brought to bear. For in these days to come the beast will be joined by Anti-Christ, who will burn with rage, and vent his displeasure on Christ's followers. Also the barbarism and savage disposition of the Pagans will be let loose. Then will the dragon tear and destroy. This will, indeed, be a day or time of visitation. The political disturbances will be terrible. Nation against nation plotting and deceiving; internal strife and outward dangers. These are of a kind to appal one in reading them. Then come the temporal or physical evils. These are to be a horrible train of ills in the form of pestilence, famine, and earthquakes. The plague of yellow fever is as nought to some of the scourges that will then go forth. Gibbon, the historian, tells of a plague that swept away two-thirds of Europe and Asia. At that time the dead lay unburied by thousands. In Constantinople, for three months, five and even ten thousand persons died daily. The famines in India and China give us some idea of those yet to come. Of the earthquakes, such as have been will be repeated in increasing terror, violence, and destruction. To all these shall be added fire from heaven, hail, whirlwinds, and floods. These are times that will try men's souls. Read the prophets for yourselves, and range yourselves on the Lord's sake.

WONDERS OF THE FUTURE.
Discourse XV.
Purpose of the Flood—The Abrahamic Current—Rending Mount Olivet—Former Earthquakes—Boundaries of Palestine—Dan and Gad to Guard the "Gates"—Gad the Scotchman—The Future Jerusalem—The Dead Sea and Mediterranean to be Joined—Mistake of Spiritualising Everything.

"And His feet shall stand in that day upon the Mount of Olives, which is before Jerusalem on the East; and the Mount of Olives shall cleave in the midst thereof toward the East and toward the West, and there shall be a very great valley; and half the mountain shall remove toward the North, and half of it toward the South."—Zech. xiv. 4.

SOME four thousand years ago the earth was washed with the regenerating waters of a terrible flood. Millions were suddenly cut off, with their handiwork and antediluvian civilisation. The swelling floods subsided, and the God-avenging waters retired to their appointed place. The earth again stood forth in virgin strength, lonely, bare, and cityless, but with a potency and promise inviting and grand. Across these swelling floods one craft has been safely borne; in it was stored the seed-stock of a new world of man and beast. The destruction had been complete and terrible. If we credit Dr. Gurney and others who have written on this subject, the population far exceeded the inhabitants of to-day. But whether they did or did not, we know that many must have perished, and civilisation must have been hurled back to a primitive beginning. No doubt the present seas and oceans cover over the ruins of that age. Eliphaz, the Temanite, when addressing Job, said: "Hast thou marked the old way, which wicked men have trodden, which were cut down out of time? *whose foundation was overflown with a flood?*" Now is it not reasonable to suppose that in this and every other great change in nature God has a purpose —a design agreeable with His own exalted character? He is too wise to err, and too good to be unkind. The flood came for the same reason that He only gave Adam one wife. And what was that reason? It was that He might fill the world with a godly seed. "And did not He make one? Yet had He the residue of the Spirit. And wherefore one? That He might seek a godly seed" (Mal. ii. 15). The same Spirit which made one Eve could have made twenty, for the residue of the Spirit was with Him. It was in the interest of morality and godliness that the flood came.

When this design began to fail of being accomplished by the increased wickedness of the post-diluvians, then God called Abram, and through Abraham and his seed designed that this purpose should flow on and be fulfilled. Through this Abrahamic channel flow all the purposes of a Divine Providence in this world. Through his seed all the nations of the earth are to be blessed. The children of Abraham are the appointed and divinely authorised agents of God. Through them, as primary, He has, and is, and will evangelise the world. Abraham stands to the generations of earth as the Gulf-stream to Europe and the isles of the sea. This Gulf-stream is our largest river; being the longest, broadest, and deepest. Its bottom and banks are cold water. Compressed by the straits of Florida, it rushes forth to warm and replenish the earth and isles of the sea. So the forces of a Divine Providence compressed in Abraham go forth to bless mankind. The Gulf-stream is water in water, and Abraham's seed are men among men. Providence is at once clear and intelligible, and history is at once plain, reasonable, and harmonious, when interpreted in harmony with the Abrahamic covenant. The scattering and returning of Israel and Judah to Palestine, and the intervening history, from the time of dispersion to the Return, is clear as noonday. Their location, oppression, prosperity and victories, have long been foretold by prophets inspired of God.

Through all the changes in nature God has a design. He prepared the world for Adam and his seed, and he did so by some wonderful upheaving and overturning; this scientists will admit. This world, in its present shape and condition, indicates fierce and protracted struggles. The outlines of strange and sublime revolutions are imprinted on her rock-ribbed bosom. Look at her cloud-capped mountains, her snow-crowned peaks, her wild and rocky wastes, her barren plains and sandy deserts, her fruitful hills and luxuriant valleys, her mighty oceans and swelling seas, her inland lakes and rolling rivers; these tell us of a time long ago—of the time when the Mighty One went forth to work a work, to build a house and make a home for His creature, man. And as it was necessary in the preparatory stage to tune nature to the coming man, so all along through the history of the centuries we find nature holding a subordinate relation to man. The world is not run on one principle and man on another, but both are permeaated by a divine force and led on to a divine end. All things are ours, and we are Christ's, and Christ is God's; this is the established order of subordination. Most certainly it cannot be unscientific in the Author of nature to make the same His messenger for good or evil. It is not unscientific to throw a line from the shore to a ship in distress, even though thrown from the mouth of a cannon, nor is it counted unscientific to use that same cannon in war to destroy men.

The earthquake spoken of in the text is, indeed a small affair in comparison to some that have occurred in this world; and if the same God be living now as then, surely He can rend in twain the little mountain of Olivet. And if we grant to the infidel scientist of to-day the fact that there is no God, still the thing prophesied of is neither unreasonable or impossible, because what has been may be again; and as the demand in this case is small in comparison to what has been, surely this thing may come to pass. In times past Providence and the wants of the Church have been timely aided by convulsions in nature, and if they were only so accidentally, why then accidentally they may all agree again. To the scientist, especially the geologist, there can be no great difficulty in crediting the miracles of the text when we think of the successive revolutions that have taken place. Fires, and floods, and earthquakes, have done sublime service in the past, whether we credit the same to Nature or to God. That an earthquake, or any peculiar expression of Nature, should be timed to meet a special condition of the Church or the special purposes of a Providence, is not strange. In such an event there really is no more wonder than that a man should set an alarm on his clock to go off at three minutes past four in the morning. Some men can swallow big things if you will only allow them to make out the author to be Nature. But whether we attribute the things past to Nature or to God, we know that wonderful things have happened.

Seismology, the science of earthquakes, is by no means void of interest. The earthquake catalogue of the British Association takes notice of, and records the occurrence of, over 6,000 that happened between 1606 B.C. and 1842 A.D. Some of these have been terrible in force, destruction, and extent, oftentimes changing the whole face of a country, its climate, and river courses. The great earthquake of 1783, in Calabria, probably caused the death of 100,000 people; it was felt over a great part of Europe. The city of Lisbon was visited on the morning of November 1st, 1755, with an earthquake so severe that in a few minutes 60,000 persons perished and most of the city was destroyed and buried beneath the water of the bay, some 600 feet.

The country given to Abraham embraces all of what we call

Syria. It is central, and specially adapted for the future purposes of God through Abraham's seed. Beginning with the North-west corner, the boundaries will be Mount Taurus, River Euphrates, Persian Gulf, Arabian Sea, Red Sea, River Nile, and Mediterranean, enclosing Syria, Arabia Deserts, Arabia Felix and Arabia Petœa. Thus it will be seen that the Abrahamic inheritance is surrounded by water, except at two points—namely, the North-west land boundary, which is between the Euphrates and the Mediterranean Sea. The entrance is through the mountain range of Taurus, and forms a natural gate or mountain pass from Europe and Asia into Palestine. Here, when the Tribes are re-settled in the land of Palestine, this gate will be in the allotment of Dan. Our Irish brethren will again be in the North-West, where they will have to fight and defend the land and the truth, as in the days of old, for their brethren. The fact is, " Dan shall judge his people as one of the Tribes of Israel," said old Jacob. The judge in olden times sat in the gate. So will Dan sit. Moses said that Dan was a lion's whelp. Among Israel it is customary to put lions as guards at gateways. The South-west corner, between the Mediterranean and the Sea of Suez, forms the other land boundary. Through this gate will come the teeming millions of Africa. At this gate will be the Tribe of Gad—that is, a portion of the Scotch, the Lowlanders. The Tribes will be hemmed in one by another so that they cannot enlarge their territory; but Gad can, for a vast country opens up beyond the gate. It is barren; still the desert is to blossom as a rose. Of Gad it was said by Moses, " Blessed be He that enlargeth Gad; he dwelleth as a lion and teareth the arm with the crown of the head. And he provided the first part for himself, because there, in a portion of the lawgiver, was he seated." You remember that Sinai is in this portion. What sight and foresight Jacob and Moses had! The land as thus bounded would be 600 miles broad from the Red Sea to the River

Euphrates, and 1,390 between the Red Sea and Persian Gulf, and from the Mediterranean to the Arabian Sea 1,600. These boundaries you will glean by taking note of the several promises to Abraham and his seed, as recorded in Gen. xv. 10, and Exod. xxiii. 31, and Deut. xi. 24. The land so promised and given specially to Abraham and his seed, the descendants of Abraham never yet occupied; no, not half of it, even in the palmy days of King Solomon. Will it ever be? We answer, Yes, as sure as the seasons and night and day. He is faithful that has promised, and will do it.

This remarkable peninsular will be the theatre of the future glory of Israel and Judah. As finely described by the Rev. A. B. Grimaldi, it will be found to be most exactly and suitably placed to enable them to fulfil their high destiny to all nations, and become the centre of all lands, the praise and beauty of the whole earth. This land has, in fact, a central position for communication, commerce, and all other advantages of civilization not enjoyed by any other portion of land in the whole world; while the peculiar geographical formation is such that it has an immense sea-board, and is therefore fitted for vaster commercial and naval operations than have ever yet been seen, commanding, as it does, the three most important seas and the two largest rivers of the whole world.

This land, as laid out by Ezekiel, will be divided into thirteen longitudinal strips, sixty miles long, and twenty broad. In the very centre will be a portion, some fifty miles square, which will be divided and apportioned to what is called the holy oblation—namely, in the very middle will be the temple, a mile square, or larger than ever the whole city of Jerusalem has yet been. Then the city will be ten miles square. On one side will be a portion for the priests; on another, a portion for the Levites; and on the other two sides, the prince's or king's portion. This portion, which will be on the East and West sides, will be sixty miles long by ten broad, or some 600 miles square. But it is clear he will need it, for he will not be supported by taxes. He will have to judge the land. He cannot take any more land. He will have to support his own family. No public grant to his children. He will have to be liberal with the temple. He will have sixty miles of sea coast to defend and sixty miles of land frontier to protect, and thus cover some of the weaker tribes. The city will have 720 square miles as a suburb, in which to raise supplies specially for itself. It will in reality be in two parts—one called by the prophets the profane; here will the commercial business be done. The other part will be sacred. Into it strangers will not enter; it will be holy—a quiet habitation. "There the glorious Lord will be unto us a place of broad rivers and streams, wherein shall go no galley with oars, neither shall gallant ships pass thereby." The city proper will be some thirty miles North of the present city of Jerusalem.

NINETEEN HUNDRED AND FIFTY-SEVEN.
Discourse XVI.

"Signs of the Times"—The Return to Jerusalem—Forces of Russia and England—Present Locality of Ancient Nations—Origin of American Republicanism—Federation of the Nations Coming—Evolution and Devolution.

"Blessed is he that waiteth, and cometh to the thousand three hundred and five and thirty days."--Dan. xii. 12.

So according to the prophet Daniel there is a time to come in which it will be blessed to live. The prophecies of Daniel are generally of a material character—that is, they have special reference to this world politically, and to this end he had direct and special reference to certain kingdoms in existence at the time of writing, as well as others that were to come into being. Of all the prophets he concerns himself the most with positive data of the rise and fall of nations. The figures of the data used, we freely confess, are difficult to understand and interpret. The Church and times are greatly in need of some man competent on this point. All prophetic students know the diversity and confusion in this department of theology. Of all the difficult departments of theology none exceed the numerical. The numerical symbolism of the Bible is as yet but little understood. True, indeed, we are improving. Aided by Providence, we are enabled to interpret some dates by data —that is, certain events occuring locate us and point out the prophetic period we are in. Like the captain who is unable by his certain and usual modes of calculating to find his whereabouts, does so by currents, the Gulf-stream, islands, colour of water, &c., did we know the exact quantity of Daniel's two thousand and three hundred days, his times, time, and half a time, his seventy weeks, his thousand two hundred and ninety days, and the thousand three hundred and five and thirty days, then we could deal with the prophecies with a definitiveness to which as yet we are strangers.

The times, however, are peculiarly interesting from the very fact that the Church is waking up to the importance of prophetic study. "Coming events cast their shadows before," is a trite but true saying, and here as true as anywhere. Men feel in their fears and hopes the pressure of prophecy. The Church is remarkably anxious and unrest. Governments are suspicious and confused. The populace are restless and threatening. Indeed, everything conspires in Church, State, and people to forecast the future. A thunderstorm is felt before it is seen or heard. It shadows the mind, thrills the nerves, and pains the rheumatic limbs. Many in 1858 felt war coming in our own country. Many were at a loss to interpret their fears. Some, however, interpreted the signs of the times and sounded an alarm.

The few years to come are pregnant with angry forces. Men are busy in Russia, Germany, France, England, and America, sowing the winds, and the harvest will surely be whirlwinds. But, beyond all, the sky is clear. War ceases, commerce revives, the nations accept a settled peace, science and religion join hand in hand to prepare the wastes and woes of war. The beast is overcome, Anti-Christ is slain, and the dragon is banished from the earth. Jerusalem again rises in splendour from the grave of desolation. Again Canaan will become the glory of all lands, and Jerusalem the glory of Canaan. Here, again, after centuries of wandering, shall the throne of David find rest, and on it one of David's seed, chosen and anointed of God, accepted of men, and served by the nations. Crowned and Imperial Salem shall become the home of her long-captive sons and daughters. Israel and Judah shall meet together, and shall be one stick, one people, having one head, one throne, one city, one Lord, even Jesus. "Therefore, they shall come and sing in the height of Zion, and shall flow together to the goodness of the Lord, for wheat, and for wine, and for oil, and for the young of the flock and of the herd; and their soul shall be as a watered garden, and they shall not sorrow any more at all" (Jeremiah xxxi. 12).

No one can read the prophecies that find their fulfilment after the battle of Armageddon—or, as the prophets have it, "after those days," without being ravished with delight. Israel in her palmy days, and Judah in her glory! A nation called of God, and ruled by God through David or Solomon; how inviting! When Heaven was their Defence and Provider; when the fidelity of men to God was enough of defence, and the morality of a people was a rich manure giving an abundant harvest in field, stall, and orchard; then we see the true position of a nation, its grandeur and prosperity. I am convinced that morality has a more intimate relation with the forces and wealth of nature than we are in the habit of believing. God can give increased measure to the harvest, fruitfulness to the vine, plenty in the orchard, increase in the stall, and addition to the household. Time upon time are these blessings promised by the prophets to Israel and Judah in the latter day.

Take notice of a few statements of the prophets responding to those times—the times that will ensue after the Ten Lost Tribes of Israel and the Jews are again possessed of, and settled in, Palestine. Jeremiah, in the 30th chapter and 31st, refers to those times: "For lo, the days come, saith the Lord, that I will bring again the captivity of My people, Israel and Judah, saith the Lord; and I will cause them to return to the land that I gave to their fathers, and they shall possess it"—referring to this time and the battle of Armageddon, in which Israel will be tested, as we have before shown. "Alas! for that day is great, so that none is like it; it is even the time of

NINETEEN HUNDRED AND FIFTY-SEVEN.   153

Jacob's trouble; but he shall be saved out of it." Now, we ask, why will it be specially a time of trouble? We answer, because of the strength of the combined forces that will be arrayed against Israel—that is, England. The forces, as set forth in the Scriptures, are *thirteen on one side,* led by Russia, and *four on the other,* which will be led by England. The *thirteen* are: 1st, Gog; 2nd, Magog; 3rd, Rosh; 4th, Meshech; 5th, Tubal; 6th, Persia; 7th Ethiopia; 8th, Libya; 9th, Gomer; 10th, Togarmah; 11th, the Beast; 12th, the Dragon; and 13th, Anti-Christ. The *four* are: 1st, Sheba; 2nd, Dedan; 3rd, Merchants of Tarshish with all their young lions; 4th, the Jews and Israelites settled in Palestine, that will not be led astray by Anti-Christ.

To understand the prophets when forecasting the future, we must keep in mind that in speaking of a nation's destiny in the future, they would speak of it by the name it had at that time, if such a nation had an existence at that time. But in course of time, such nations would change their name, and sometime locality; in such a case they must be found. For instance, if one desires to know the destiny of Turkey, he will find it set forth by the prophets under the name of Edom and Esau. Moab and Ammon are found in the Poles and Hungarians; they were the sons of Lot. In all parts of the world the children of Abraham have an attachment for each other. Thus India was peopled at first by the descendants of Abraham; hence they will mix with, and accept English rule sooner than any other people. "But unto the sons of the concubines which Abraham had, Abraham gave gifts, and sent them away from Isaac his son while he yet lived, Eastward, unto the East country" (Gen. xxv. 6.). If we trace back the origin of a people to their head or founder, we will better understand their peculiarities and national idiosyncracies. Study Ishmael to understand the Arabs, Esau to understand the Turks, Ammon and Moab to understand the Poles and Hungarians.

Study the character and condition of Manasseh in Egypt, as being brought up in a palace, and being the lawful heir, but deprived of his birthright by a Providence which he could not understand, and you have at once a key to the Pilgrim character, and the characteristics of a real American—why he hates titles, kings, and aristocracies. But he forgets not the place of his youth when he had the great seal made; for on the reverse of the great seal of the United States you will have the figure of a Pyramid crowned with the All-seeing eye. No tribe but the tribe of Manasseh could say, or did say, "We are a great people." Yet so this tribe said to Joshua (see Josh. xvii.). So we often say, "We are a great people."

Rachel and Leah, the two wives of Jacob, are the real source of the separation of the Ten Tribes of Israel from Judah. Each wife sought to have her son as a leader. Thus between Judah and Joseph began the spirit of rivalry. Ephraim took up the cause of Rachel. David and Saul's bitterness lies here. David stood for Leah, and Saul for Rachel. The descendants of the North of Ireland, being from the Tribe of Dan, have ever been distinct from the rest of the Irish in features, enterprise, spirit and religion; for the others are the Canaanites of old, the Philistines.

Who do the thirteen enemies stand for to-day? Let me answer you briefly. Gog stands for the Caucasians, or mountain tribes of Caucasus. Magog covers the inhabitants and country North of the Caucasian mountains, and they are known as Tartars. Rosh, or Roosh; means the real Russians. Their ruler is called by the prophet Ezekiel *Nasi Roosh*. We translate it the chief prince of Meshech. This portion or people of Russia, are the old Babylonians, hence the hate and rivalry between England and that nation. Meshech means the Muscovites, who made Moscow what it is. Tubal is found in the Siberians. Meshech and Tubal are generally mentioned together in the Scriptures, and, strange to say, they are found together in history to-day. Moscow is the capital of Meshech, for though to the world St. Petersburgh seems to be, yet every imperial document is signed and dated Moscow. Tobolski is the capital of Tubal or Siberia. Persia still retains its ancient name, and will be easily recognised. Also the same with Ethiopia. Lybia takes in a portion of the African race. Gomer stands for the Germans in part, for those who descended from Gomer. From this word Gomer is Gomeron, Gemren, and the country Germia, hence, Germany and Germans. Togarmah includes the people of Independent Tartary. The Dragon includes China. The Beast, the Jesuits, and their followers, which will take in France, Spain, Italy, and South America; and at first divide even England, especially Ireland, and the United States. Anti-Christ will be chiefly sustained by the Jews, who will have been settled in Palestine.

The four opposing forces led by England: Sheba represents India, who is already training for this time of battle. Dedan embraces Arabia, especially that part occupied by the Sultan of Muscat. Merchants of Tarshish and all the young lions means England and her colonies, in which is embraced the United States. Manasseh will have to stretch out a helping hand to Jacob in the time of his trouble, for she cannot allow liberty to be enslaved, and freedom of worship and conscience to be trampled under foot. The plague will come here sooner than we think, by a civil and internal division among ourselves, which will force us to take part. The Jews that are not carried away with Anti-Christ will join with their brethren of Israel. The called, the chosen, and the faithful, will be one party, and they will be on the Lord's side.

If during the late Turkish war we could have had our despatches agreeable to ancient names of people and country, they would have sounded queer. Instead of reading of the Russians passing the Caucasus, and moving upon Erzeroum by way of Kars, we should have read: " Rapid advance of the

Babylonians under the chief prince of Meshech. Successful passage of the Pison. The whole land of Havilah occupied. The men of Togarmah rally at Gihon. Fierce fighting in Eden. The invaders defeated in the mountains of Ararat." For according to ancient names of people and country, such was the fact. It is comforting to all God's people to know from His Word that there is a time of peace; that there is a golden age in the near future. Dr. McKay has the Christian idea in his poem:—

> "There is a good time coming, boys,
> Wait a little longer;
> Let us aid it all we can,
> Every woman, every man,
> The good time coming."

When will the 1,335 days of years, spoken of in the text, end? We answer, About the year 1957. And why that year? Because these days evidently date there, beginning from the time the daily sacrifice is taken away and the city trodden under foot. The little goat horn of Daniel viii. 9 stands, we have before shown you, for Turkey. "And out of one of them came forth a little horn, which waxed exceeding great toward the South, and toward the East, and toward the pleasant land." It stands for Mahommedanism, which was to overturn Christianity for a given period, a time, times, and a half time, or in figures, 1260. Now Mahommed was accepted and crowned at Mecca in the year 622. If we add 1260 and 622, we have 1882—a time that is very plainly pointed out in the Pyramid. Daniel says, "Seventy weeks are determined upon Thy people and upon Thy holy city," Jerusalem. These weeks put into prophetic years make 490, which, of course, brings us to the time when Jerusalem was destroyed by Titus. Daniel asked how long the vision concerning the daily sacrifice and transgression of desolation to give the sanctuary and people to be trodden down? The answer was, Unto 2,300 days, taking a day for a year.

Jerusalem was destroyed in the year 70. Take this from 490 and we have 420. Now these 420 years taken from 2,300 will bring 1880. Then the sanctuary is to be cleansed.

In the twelfth chapter of Daniel, eleventh verse, we find thirty days added to the 1,260, making 1,290; these added thirty years denote the time England will have to contend for her right to Palestine. It will be finally acknowledged, however, by all nations. In 1935 the battle of Armageddon will end, but Palestine will not be fully settled down to a peaceful possession till 1957. Then the government will be fully established and acknowledged all over the world. The kings and Gentile nations will have gone up to Jerusalem and given in their adherence. Then all the world will be federated to David's throne. The year 1957 I arrive at by the same rule as the other—1,335, when added to 622, makes 1,957. " Blessed," says Daniel, " are they who see that time."

The world is to undergo some marvellous changes these next few years—mechanically, politically, socially, and morally; the telephone, the phonograph, the microphone, the telemachole and coming improvements will transform our modes of labour and learning beyond our present conception. God times inventions and improvements to the advancement of His kingdom.

I do not regard inventions as mere accidents, but as the outcoming of a divine intent through human agencies. Watts and Wesley both did good service for the Church and the world. Edison and others of kindred minds are scientific prophets. "The earth is the Lord's, and the fulness thereof." All is made subservient to the progress of the kingdom of heaven. The doctrine of the evolution of man, as taught by the late Dr. Darwin is neither complimentary to man or God; but the doctrine of devolution is. Man is a developing creature—a creature who takes centuries to grow in. The devolution of God is through man by means of all the increasing facilities and agencies that make man stronger, wiser, and better. The secret powers and forces of nature are revealed to man in the ratio of his ability to apply them, on the same scale as we instruct our children.

In the latter days, or the period spoken of by Daniel, nature will be divinely prompted with an impulse of generosity not now known, for then men will be wise enough, strong enough, and good enough, to use the same and not abuse. The prophetic teachings glow with promises of regaling plenty, peace, and good will in those days. " I will multiply upon you man and beasts; and they shall increase and bring fruit ; and I will settle you after your old estates, and will do better unto you than at your beginnings; and ye shall know that I am the Lord." (Ezek. xxxvi. 11). Again : " I will multiply the fruit of the tree, and the increase of the field, that ye receive no more reproach of famine, among the heathen." I submit and believe that all this God will do by what men are pleased to call natural law. The divine will not rudely break in upon His own established laws.

Sin impairs the energy and growth of man, and so infringes upon Nature. As man frees himself from the bondage and sequences of sin, he will rise higher and higher in his command and authority over Nature's forces. Three several times the earth has been cursed, which curse is gradually removed as man returns unto his God in loving and obedient service. " And now art thou cursed from the earth, which hath opened her mouth to receive thy brother's blood from thy hand. When thou tillest the ground, it shall not henceforth yield unto thee her strength" (Gen. iv. 11). The secret of a world's wealth and peace lies here, and it were well if reformers and agitators understood this. For they work best who work in harmony with God and His laws.

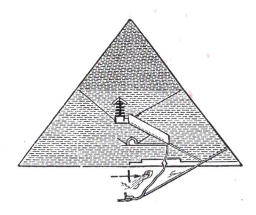

"In that day there shall be an altar to the Lord in the midst of the land of Egypt, and a pillar at the border thereof to the Lord; and it shall be for a sign, and for a witness unto the Lord of hosts in the land of Egypt."—Isaiah xix. 19.

THE STONE WITNESS.*
Discourse XVII.

The Great Pyramid—Who Job was—Who built the Pyramid—What it was Built for—An Epitome of the Earth—The History of Man Contained in it, Past and Future—Science and the Bible, etc. etc.

UNDER the organ gallery, behind the pulpit, was a representation of the Pyramid, or as the learned doctor terms it, "the stone Bible," its massive rectangular dark stone foundation, and some of the most interesting of its interior passages, chambers, and mysteries. All eyes were fastened in scrutiny upon it, well knowing that some revelation of unusual Christian interest would be made by the Doctor from it as soon as his lecture commenced. The preliminary exercises of singing by a well-trained choir and

---

* This Discourse we give to the reader as reported. In all the others we have excluded the reporter's introduction and personal references.

prayer were therefore impatiently listened to by many whose thoughts were concentrated on the wonders of the Pyramid and its astounding confirmation of the prophetic Scriptures. Dr. Wild read a lesson from Job xxxviii., remarking that the author of that book was also the engineering director or architectural author of the Pyramid, and identical with Shem and Melchisedec. The book of Job is the oldest book in the world by 200 or 300 years. Shem, or Job, was ninety-eight years old when he entered the ark, and he lived thirty years after Abraham, with whom therefore he shook hands, as well as with Methusaleh, who shook hands with Adam. Only one man, therefore, stood between Adam and Shem, and only two, or not quite two, between Adam and Abraham. The book of Berosus, of Babylon, is the only one that compares with Job in antiquity. This was the age of tradition, before Moses compiled the first portions of it. In the days of Abraham, Shem was the patriarch, or oldest, of his family; and it was therefore to him he did homage, according to the patriarchal custom, under the name of Melchisedec, when returning from the slaughter of the kings. Shem had brought with him from the days before the Flood much of the knowledge and wisdom which had been accumulated in the earth during the 2,000 years previous to that event, and which was swept away when only eight perons were saved in the ark. We have been told that the human race has gradually improved, and that our ancestors in far-off ages were monkeys, or something of that sort, but the remains of the ruins, and knowledge of antiquity, show everything the reverse of this to be the truth. Look at that Pyramid. We could not build it to-day, with all our boasted science. It will bear in every respect the closest scientific scrutiny. Our greatest scientists are only beginning to comprehend the depths of its mysteries, yet it is over 4,000 years old. The capstone on top of it is a Pyramid in itself, in minature, unlike anything of the kind or any other building on the earth. The reverend gentleman then continued to read from Job. xxxviii., and show that the writer of it was master of astronomical and geographical science and the builder of the Pyramid, which is a miniature of the measurement of the earth, and indicates the history of the human race. After this preliminary dissertation, he took for his text Isaiah xxviii. 29: "This also cometh forth from the Lord of hosts, which is wonderful in counsel, and excellent in working."

The Bible is a growing Book, being more read and better understood as the years pass by; and as men shall increase in knowledge and power, so the Bible will gain in influence and authority. Opposition to its teaching, and vaunting denial of its authority shall be made subservient to its interests by goading on the Church to a wiser and more noble defence and exposition of the same. No theology can levy upon the well-defined facts of science in confirmation of the sublime teachings of inspiration. The Christian student need not hold himself in timid dread for fear the scientist will discover aught in the realms of nature that will contradict the Word of God: for as sure as God is the Author of both, so surely shall we find an agreement between revelation and science at every point truly understood—increased light means increased evidence. Nations and men, nature and providence, are united witnesses for God and the Scriptures; and the more we know of the past, the better shall we understand the present and forecast the future. Let us recognise the future. Let us recognise the important difference between the Bible subjectively and objectively—that is, between what the Bible really is and what men think it is. Let us be free enough, bold enough, and wise enough to claim the Bible itself. Let us unyoke it from tradition, which claims to be superior, or even equal. Let us divorce it from councils, from creeds, from sects and denominations; let us lift it up out of the ecclesiastical rut of ages. Let us with a commendable pride count ourselves worthy and able to formulate our own creeds, make our own prayers and confessions, accounting that the liberties of our fathers have been bequeathed to their children, and that the same God who gave them liberty and power is no less gracious to us, their offsprings. Traditions, councils, creeds, and degrees are worth much unto us as aids to a higher life and a nobler civilisation. The Christian fathers, the Luthers, Calvins, Knoxes, Wesleys, and others, were our servants, as we will be the servants of coming generations. They worked grandly, they wrought well, they procured for us a goodly heritage; to them we are indebted. Yet it was not their purpose nor the design of Providence to enslave us, or to stereotype the Church for the ages to come. Increased light is increased evidence, enabling us the better to understand the Word of God. When a publisher has stereotyped a book he is naturally loth to make any change or correction; so Churches who have stereotyped the Bible are very unwilling to change, to receive light. Hence, they are sometimes found opposing the march of a better civilization, providing and sustaining all manner of institutions and tyrannies: the torturing and terrible Inquisition of Spain, the punishment and hanging of supposed witches by England and New England, the bondage and slavery of the South. So, to prove their creeds and systems correct, they each have a mode of their own, Catholic, Episcopalian, Baptist, Congregational, Methodist, &c. *So also,* theologians have often been impatient to reconcile the Scriptures with history, even to suggest mistakes in the sacred record. Instance Daniel being made the THIRD RULER. *They supposed it meant second,* but later researches show that Babylon had two rulers at that time—namely, Nebuchadnezzar and Belshazzar—so Daniel was made a third. See the remains of Borsippa, near Babylon (Dan. v. 29). Now, we know that both Daniel and Berosus, the old Babylonian historians, were right, and the Bible was right in using the word third. God, in His revelation has always been equal to man's need. Tradition—Abraham saw Shem, for Shem lived some thirty years after Abraham's death. Shem, and Melchisedek, and Job, are likely the same person. Certainly, Shem and Melchisedek are the same, and by Egyptian historians called Philitis. This Philitis was the builder of the Great Pyramid. Now Shem saw Methuselah and Methusaleh Adam. Thus, then, tradition would be sufficient. As tradition failed, the written Word began. There is little doubt now but that *Shem* called also Melchisedek, was the builder of the Pyramid, being instructed of God as his father Noah had been in building the ark, and Moses with the tabernacle, and Solomon with the temple, as the prophet in the text and context shows that the wisdom of the man is often the gift of God. *See Moses also.* "And the Lord spake unto Moses saying, See, I have called by name Bezaleel, the son of Uri, the son of Hur, of the Tribe of Judah; and I have filled him with the Spirit of God, in wisdom, and in understanding and in knowledge, and in all manner of workmanship: to devise cunning works, to work in gold, and in silver, and in brass, and in cutting of stones, to set them, and in carving of timber, to work in all manner of workmanship. And, behold, I have given him Aholiab, the Son of Ahisamach, of the Tribe of Dan; and in the hearts of all that are wise-hearted I have put wisdom that they may make all that I have commanded thee " (Exodus xxxi. 1—6).

Let us look at this building, for it is a special revelation for these times. For this precise and scientific day God has provided. Science and the Bible are interlocked in this building; they agree, they testify for the same God, yet they witness to the same Christ, the Providence and history of His chosen people. This stone book could not be read till now; it even takes the most precise scientific men of the day to read it. For thousands of years there has been no one in the court of the world able to question and interpret this witness of the Lord in Egypt. The scientists have been asking for some other revelation than the Bible, for the supernatural in a scientific form, for something beyond man, for something all could see, for something that would answer to pure science, for something that could be seen, handled, measured, tested, and amenable to mathematics; something superhuman, for something in which the human and the Divine blend. Thank Heaven, all they ask is granted in this stone monument. Here we have science forecast for thousands of years; here we have the grandest of problems in science solved, and the sublimest phenomena of religion and science crystalised, symbolising and teaching the most marvellous facts in religion, sociology, and astronomy. It is not a tomb, nor granary, nor temple, but a pillar and witness unto the Lord of hosts. Think of a few facts. 1. Its location, the centre of the land surface of the whole earth. Hence the best zero point on earth for meridional and latitudinal calculations. Central to clime—here is no rust, moss, nor frosts to destroy, nor earthquake—a well-chosen spot for such a pillar. It form and size—symbolising the earth quantity in its weight of five millions of tons—the freight of 1,250 of the largest steamers leaving New York. Its shape, or inclination from base to apex, the same as from the pole to the equator. To express this the builder sloped it ten feet for every nine in height. On this building the sun can shine upon the whole of it twice a year without a shadow. This building is the most correctly orient of any structure on the earth. It is the highest, largest, and oldest building on earth, rising to the height of 486 feet and a fraction, which height if multiplied by ten nine times gives the distance of the earth from the sun, or pile a thousand million pyramids one on the other, and the last would touch the sun. As it stood perfect it was the circle squared; for the height is the radius of a circle, whose circumference, if divided into four equal parts, each part would equal one of the surface sides of the base—closer in approximation than Walli's Indivisibles, or Newton's Fluxions, or

Liebnitz's Calculus. The door of entrance was some forty-nine feet from its base, and 300 inches East of the centre, so as at once to express the tilt of the earth's axis from the plane of its orbit, and by its height from the ground express the Precession of the Equinoxes. What a witness outwardly, when complete, of polished marble, covering some thirteen and a-half acres, within and without clean and free from idolatrous marks. But God foretold the place and purpose of this huge pile through the prophet Isaiah (xix. 19, 20): "In that day shall there be an altar to the Lord in the midst of the land of Egypt, and a pillar at the border thereof to the Lord. And it shall be for a sign and for a witness unto the Lord of hosts in the land of Egypt." Here we see the *altar* and *pillar* are *one* and the same, and a scientific fact is expressed when the prophet says it shall be in the midst and on the border. The position of the Pyramid is such, being at the sector point of Upper and Lower Egypt, thus being on the border of both, yet in the midst. The sector point of the arm is where the wrist joins the hand. The spreading hand represents Lower, and the arm Upper Egypt. (See on frontispiece the sector plate.)

May we ask what the pillar and witness—the Pyramid— has to say on the Jewish question, for it has not left this fact unnoticed? At the junction of the first ascending passage with the Grand Gallery, on the left-hand side, or East, there is a horizontal passage-way leading to what is called the Queen's Chamber. This Chamber is on the twenty-fifth course of masonry. Now, it is allowed, the Grand Gallery expresses the time of Christ's advent and fulness of time—enlarged liberty. The ascending passage being only four feet high, men were cramped in passing up, but on reaching the Grand Gallery they were free, for it is twenty-eight feet high.

The passage to the Queen's Chamber is only four feet, and is it not strange that it is altogether Jewish? This low horizontal passage terminates in a grand Sabbatic room, which symbolises the Jewish Sabbath-week, feasts, and time periods.

From this passage we learn that the Jews rejected Christ, and went off by themselves, refusing the liberty of Christ. So as truly as the coming of Christ had been forecast in this Pyramid, so had His rejection by the Jews.

The very mortar in this chamber is mixed with salt. The chamber is seven sided. The last seventh of the passage-way sinks down, giving more room to move in. Salt was an article used freely with the Jews in sacrificing. Seven was a sacred number. The sinking of the last seventh part of the passage-way floor may mean the enlarging privilege of the Jews in this latter day. Of the civilised nations, only Russia and Spain forbid them citizenship. Even Turkey admits them now as citizens.

The Jews have been represented as being blind in part. The passage-way and chamber have been difficult to explore because of foul air, there being no ventilating tubes as in the King's Chamber.

But, strange to say, a gentleman exploring this chamber a short time ago, found two tubes by an accident in striking the side wall with a hammer. The tubes had been left entirely closed over with a thin unbroken scale. These tubes extended inward through the masonry, and into the stones forming the walls of the room, all nicely cut, but for about one inch they were not cut through into the room itself. Thus the whole was designed is evident. This thin scale no doubt symbolises the condition of the Jew. His eyes are now open, the time of his wanderings nearly spent, as told by this Pyramid.

The curses foretold upon the Jews have been terribly fulfilled. So shall the blessings foretold now in reserve. It was foretold that he would reject Christ; so he did. But it is also foretold that he will yet look upon Him whom he pierced, and mourn and repent, and accept the true Messiah. Lo-ruhamah represents Lost Israel; Lo-Ammi represents cursed Judah; Ruhamah represents Israel found ; Ammi represents the curse removed from the Jews. So now we must say, as the prophet Hosea long ago instructed us—we Saxons—"Say ye unto your brother, Ammi," and you Jews, "say to your sisters, Ruhamah."

We have esteemed the Jews as cursed: we will soon esteem them blest. The Jews have never thought we were their brethren, the descendants of Abraham. But God is revealing in this latter day His own great plan; and Christ will be the Saviour of both.

"In his days Judah shall be saved, and Israel shall dwell safely. Therefore, behold, the days come, saith the Lord, that they shall no more say, The Lord liveth, which brought up the children of Israel out of Egypt; but, The Lord liveth, which brought up, and which led the seed of the House of Israel out of the North country, and from all countries whither I had driven them; and they shall dwell in their own land" (Jer. xxiii. 6—8).

Glorious times are near at hand for the Church and the world. Great things hath God promised, all of which He will in His own good time bring to pass.

The very dimensions of the doorway are of thrilling import, expressing in square inches the time of the Adamic world, which, when added to other figures, forecast the time of the end, or the 6,000 years, and point out the date of the beginning of the Millennium morn, or Sabbath of the earth—the period spoken of by Daniel when he says, "Blessed is he that waiteth, and cometh to the thousand three hundred and five and thirty days." This period we approximated in our last discourse, and made it out to be about 1,957. The doorway in square inches is 1,949; take these inches for years, and we have before the building of the Pyramid, of years 1949 A.M., time of building 2170 B.C., and length of Grand Gallery,

1,882, and we get a total of 6,001. This is indeed a close approximation.

SIGNS AND WONDERS.
Discourse XVIII.

Egypt: Past and Future—The Stone Prophet in the Wilderness—No War for Four Years—The Great Struggle to Commence in 1882—Prussia Ancient Assyria—England, Germany, and Egypt to be Allies—The Future History of the World—The Philistines the Southern Irish—Who their Great Ancestor was, &c.

"The great, the mighty God, the Lord of hosts is His name. Great in counsel, and mighty in work; for Thine eyes are open upon all the ways of the sons of men; to give every one according to his ways, and according to the fruit of his doings; which has set signs and wonders in the land of Egypt, even unto this day."—Jer. xxxii. 18—20.

EGYPT is intimately connected with Palestine in Providential history, both past, present, and future. No student can have a proper knowledge of the Jewish and Israelitish nation unless he be familiar with the early civilisation and power of Egypt. From this land went forth the Caphtorim to settle Palestine, led forth by the great and good Melchisedek, after he had built the Pyramid. Under his reign they first settled in Palestine, built and made Jerusalem their capital. On the death of Melchisedek they lost their allegiance to God, they became an idolatrous people, and were rejected by Jehovah as His special agents. They are known in after history under the name of Philistines, which simply means the followers or subjects of Philitis—a name which the early historians of Egypt gave to the builder of the Pyramid, which was none other person than Melchisedek. By the Israelites they were driven out of Palestine, and finally settled in the South of Ireland, as Irish historians allow.

Another member of the family of Shem was called—namely, Abraham, from whom came God's chosen people—Israel and the Jews. They also had to sojourn in Egypt, and they, too, were sent to Palestine, and graffed on to the purpose of God, where the Philistines had been broken off.

"Have not I brought up Israel out of the land of Egypt, and the Philistines from Caphtor?" (Amos ix. 7).

Egypt has played a noble part in the providence of God through Melchisedek, Abraham, Joseph, and Moses. Even the blessed Jesus is said to be called from this land. "Out of Egypt have I called My Son." The Egyptians gave to the world the first translation of the Hebrew Bible, and it was for centuries the stronghold of Christianity after the destruction of Jerusalem. The best of the Christian fathers were Egyptians, and in the coming struggle, the great war, which will begin * about 1882, again Egypt will become conspicuous with England. For the Germans proper are the Assyrians as the English are the Lost Tribes of Israel. Bismarck may manœuvre as he please, and be as pro-Russian as Dr. Storrs, yet when the time comes he and his people will fall in with the providential purpose, and become an ally with Israel-England; and timid and bankrupt Egypt will then come forth to take her place once more among the nations of the earth as an independent Power. Hear what the Prophet Isaiah says in chap. xix.: "And the Lord shall smite Egypt, He shall smite and heal it, and they shall return even to the Lord, and He shall be entreated of them, and shall heal them. In that day shall there be a highway out of Egypt to Assyria, and the Assyrians shall come into Egypt and the Egyptians into Assyria, and the Egyptians shall serve with the Assyrians. In that day shall

---

* This sermon was preached in 1879.

Israel be the third with Egypt and with Assyria, even a blessing in the midst of the land, whom the Lord of hosts shall bless, saying, Blessed be Egypt My people, and Assyria the work of My hands, and Israel Mine inheritance."

" IN THAT DAY " refers to this day, now at hand. To this the Great Pyramid is witness. For in verses 19 and 20 of this chapter we read : " IN THAT DAY shall there be an altar to the Lord in the midst of the Land of Egypt, and a pillar at the border thereof to the Lord. And IT shall be for a SIGN and for a WITNESS unto the Lord of hosts in the land of Egypt."

The word translated pillar is from the Hebrew word Matzaybhah, and means a large structure—some monument that is pre-eminent. The Hebrew word Ammood is translated pillar also, and corresponds to the English word pillar much better.

The word altar, in Hebrew, means lion, carrying with it the same meaning as pre-eminence. And is not this Pyramid pre-eminent? and is not the lion of monuments pre-eminent as being the oldest, pre-eminent as being the highest, pre-eminent as being the largest, pre-eminent in location—being central to all the land surface of the earth, pre-eminent in construction, unlike any other buildings, except such as have been modelled after it, pre-eminent in orientation—that is, being exactly East, North, West, and South.

Perfect orientation men in past ages and countries have tried to express in temples, churches, observatories, and monuments, yet none have succeeded so well as the Pyramid builders.

The famous Uranibourg Observatory, built by aid of the European Governments, under the skilful supervision of the learned Tycho Brahe, was found to be five minutes of a degree askew in its orientation when finished.

A few years ago our Government determined to have one perfect point of orientation, fixing upon Mount Agamenticus, in the State of Maine. They, at a great cost, and time, and labour, concluded their work, and found they were in error somewhere about the four-hundredth part of a second; although they tried to solve the problem by three distinct processes— namely, differences of zenith distance, absolute zenith distances, and by transits in prime vertical.

How then came these ancient architects so early in the world's history and progress to build so skilfully? How were they able some 4,000 years ago to find the poles, and determine the latitude and longitude so precisely? Answer, ye godless scientists, and tell us how these monkey-men were so skilled. How did they know without your instruments and instruction which parallel of latitude to choose so as to be on that line which would mark the half-way of the world's surface between the equator and the poles?

And why did they lay bare and make smooth the lime-stone table rock on which they built close to its Northern edge? Why press so closely to the brink of the hill on the North side when there was plenty of room on the South side?

Truly this witness of God is against you. In this building are "signs and wonders" even to this day, and as surely also are the eyes of Jehovah open upon all the ways of the children of men.

Know ye not that the accumulated forces and results of centuries have been bequeathed to the present generation as a legal heritage for culture and profit?

Happily for us God has not left Himself without witnesses. Long before God made bare His arm through Moses, and wrought miracles to convince Pharaoh and the Egyptians, He had wrought one miracle, a miracle which would cover the ages; not to be seen by a few only, or last for a day, but to be seen by the millions and last for centuries.

In this Pyramid we have a valuable inheritance. Its finish, its beauty, its magnitude provokes our criticism, and yet must command our admiration. This watchman on the walls of time, this sentinel in charge of the secrets and treasures of the sires of long ago, this prophet in the wilderness in rugged garb, proclaiming the will of Heaven as then made known, and now manifest, this Daniel who can interpret for us the future, this mile-stone of the ages, we do revere.

By it we are enabled to adjust our chronological dates, rectify history in some of its most important points, and judge more correctly of the attainments of our ancestors; nay, more and better, to form a truer estimate of ourselves and discern the finger of God in the manipulations of men, and an overruling Providence in the rise and fall of nations.

These signs and wonders confirm God's word, for they prove inspiration a fact; inspiration of a kind and in the very manner demanded by the unbelieving scientists. Here is a building superhuman, and of course in part supernatural, like the Bible. In this building the human and the Divine blend.

If any deny this, it remains with them to account for it, and show how a people so far back in the world's history could be so wise and learned; how they could embody so much of the sciences. One thing is certain, if the Divine had nothing to do with this building, then we are left to the conclusion that man was much superior to what the Darwinian theory admits. If void of the Divine, then the development theory is destroyed. If we admit the Divine, then it follows that inspiration is a fact.

The building is there, and it was there in the day's of Egypt's oldest historians. It has been counted as one of the seven wonders of the world.

It did not embody the ideas of the Egyptians in science, astronomy, meteorology, or religion. As their historians allow, it was built by foreigners which they hated. Nothing idolatrous was carved on it, within or without. It was a witness pure and clean. The Egyptians proclaimed and believed the earth to be square—this building proclaimed the earth round. The builders bevelled the face of the rock in a ratio of eight inches to the mile—the very quantity that science to-day admits to be the curvature of the earth—and accepts in surveying. It was their knowledge of this fact that kept the building sound, without the cracking of a joint, through centuries, though so high. The Egyptians did not use the sacred amma, or cubit, which is about twenty-five of our inches. They used a profane cubit, as Sir Isaac Newton shows.

This sacred cubit was a well and easily established proportion of the earth's diameter—the very standard now used by the English Government in surveying.

The stones of the Pyramid were twelve feet long, eight feet broad, and five deep, making twenty-five total. The building itself was a five faced figure. The Egyptians hated five. No wonder that Moses harnessed the Israelities in fives as they left Egypt, or that he should divide his book into five parts.

No wonder that the Queen's Chamber should be on the twenty-fifth course of masonry, and the King's Chamber on the fiftieth course, which is the year of jubilee, or deliverance—which year, as indicated in the Pyramid, is the year 1935.

The Egyptians calculated from the moon in their chronology. But this building takes its calculations from the sun circle. The Egyptian year was 354 days, with an intercalary month of thirty-three days added every three years.

The year embodied in the Pyramid was 365 days, five hours, forty-eight minutes, forty-seven and seven-tenths seconds. If a person took a rod of a cubit length, and measured one of the base sides of the Pyramid, he would find this twenty-five inch measure to be contained as often as there are days in the year, with the same fraction in inches as the hours, minutes, and seconds.

Is it impious to ask how these builders knew the solar year so completely? They knew the sun's circle of 448 years, which completes a circle of time without any excess or deficiency.

This they ran into weights and measures, as God's religion does. The Pyramid having four sides, would divide this circle into four parts, which make 112 pounds, or a hundred-weight; or, if multiplied by five, the faces of the Pyramid, 448 would give 2,240, or a ton.

In the descending and ascending passages a person must stoop to pass through them, but when the Grand Gallery is reached, they can stand upright, for this gallery enlarges seven times the proportion of the others. The first passages are only four feet high; this is twenty-eight.

The first ascending passage is 1,542 inches in length—the time, taking inches for years, from the exodus of Israel from Egypt to Christ.

Christ brings enlarged liberty. He was symbolised by the ton—the end of weight scale. "When the fulness of time was come God sent forth His Son."

Again, thirty-three inches in this gallery is an open sepulchre with fifty-six empty graves in miniature, carved out, telling, again, by a strange coincident, the life of years of the Saviour and His resurrection; also the number of those who rose immediately after. For the "graves were opened, and many bodies of the saints which slept arose and came out of the graves after His resurrection" (Matt. xxvii. 52).

Another remarkable feature is, that the end of this gallery the wall bulges forward about four inches, as if it were going to fall in. This gallery on the floor is 1,882 inches; on the roof, 1,878 inches. This explains to us the very times. The shadow of war—Russia and England appearing as if they would fight every day. But they know not the counsels of God, nor His sublime purpose. Surely, as the text declares, "Our God is great in counsel and mighty work; and His eyes are open upon all the ways of the sons of men." More next Sunday evening, God willing, about His own marvellous witnesses. Let us praise and adore Him.

"*And the remnant of Jacob shall be among the Gentiles, in the midst of many people, as a* LION *among the beasts of the forest, as a* YOUNG LION *among the flocks of sheep: who, if he go through, both treadeth down and teareth in pieces, and none can deliver.*"—Micah v. 7.

"*His glory is like the firstling of his bullock, and his horns like the* HORNS OF UNICORNS: *with them he shall push the people together to the* ENDS *of the* EARTH."—Deut. xxxiii. 17.

THE THRONE OF DAVID.
DISCOURSE XIX.

England's Prophecy Fulfilled in the Berlin Congress—The Harp of Tara the Harp of Israel—The Future European Alliances—Royal Succession of the House of Israel.

"I will overturn, overturn, overturn it and it shall be no more, until He comes whose right it is; and I will give it Him."—Ezek. xxi. 27.

THE closing of the famous European Congress will now freely permit us to canvass the work and results of the same, and to compare the sequences with the teachings of the prophets and intentions of Providence. The results of the Congress have taken the world by surprise. The very fact that one should have been held under the enforced conditions of the crownless king, Disraeli, was a wonder in itself. But the wonder is not confined to the meeting and work of the Congress, for outside of, and in spite of the Congress, a treaty has been made which converts wonder into amazement. Back in the middle of last May (1878), England and Turkey formed an alliance, offensive and defensive. Nay, more, for Turkey cedes to England the fruitful and strategic island of Cyprus. What a triangle of strongholds—Cyprus, Malta, and Gibraltar! Shades of Bonaparte! Where is France in these days? She is renewing her strength, and is wisely standing aside so as not to oppose Providence. In all this there is nothing new or strange to the prophetic student. For long ago it was written of Israel that she should be a company of nations, and possess the Gates of her enemies.

It is not by might, nor power of human origin, that these events must be judged, or that they come to pass. But surely by the Spirit of God. "There is a spirit in man, and the inspiration of the Almighty giveth it understanding." Here Job gives us the key to unlock the mysteries of the crownless king and his success. The apothegm of Bonaparte is as false as he was unsuccessful—namely, that Providence is always on the side of the strongest battalions. In Israel, in time of old, this was seldom true. In fact, it was not true in the experience and campaigns of Bonaparte. The logic of such a faith has been the ruin of lovely France more than once, and will be again. For it must needs be that France breaks her alliance with England, though now they are friends. France in a few years will ally with the Beast, the Roman Church, in its last struggle for rule and supremacy; and she will join hands with Anti-Christ. France will repeat the follies of '93. She will again seek to dethrone Religion, and enthrone Reason. Her Marats, Desmoulens, Herberts, Clootzes, and Robespierres are at hand ready to overturn. And the church of her choice is patiently waiting to re-enact the scenes of blood and terror of St. Bartholomew. Her time of opportunity will appear to have come in a few years. Bismarck and Kaiser William will be out of the way, and Germany will languish for want of two equal successors. And France will not forget to pay back the debt of revenge she owes to Germany, and seek to reclaim her prestige in councils, and especially to restore her lost influence over Egypt, Turkey, and the Mediterranean.

In 1878 it would not have been so easy to see how France and England were to become once again enemies. This Cyprus wedge has cleft open a little farther the dark and mysterious way.

Recently we received the astounding telegram of the treaty between England and Turkey. It evidently was a surprise, we have no doubt, even to Rev. Dr. Storrs, and the *New York Herald*, as well as to many others who could see nothing but defeat and shame for Israel-England. From Dr. Storrs we have not heard what he now thinks of his child of promise, Russia. From the *Herald* we did hear; for, by the way, the *Herald* is one of our morning papers. By an editorial of a column and a half the *Herald* struggled nobly to wriggle out of the tight corner in which its sympathies for Russia had crowded it. We like and admire the *Herald*, because of its tact and ingenuity in getting news first from any part of the world. Still this time she was behind time. Two years ago, from this pulpit, we announced the exciting facts of the past week. Last Sunday evening we closed our discourse in these words: " Now, again, England pledges herself a Continental Power, nay, more, an Asiatic power. She will come forth from the Congress the virtual ruler of Turkey, and the owner of Palestine."

If the Saxons be the Ten Lost Tribes of Israel, and most certainly they respond to all the features that were to distinctly mark them when found, as written in the Bible—then the English throne is a continuation of David's throne, and the seed on it must be the seed of David, and the inference is clear —namely, that all the blessings attaching by holy promise to

David's throne must belong to England. This is the key that unravels and makes plain the marvellous and sublime history of the English nation and throne. We know many scout the idea of the Lost Tribes ever being found, although over thirty times God declares by the prophets that they must return; surely before they return they must be found. God has not cast away His people for ever. No, no. He declares Israel to be His inheritance, and that this people He had formed for Himself.

The Two Tribes forming the Jews of to-day are said by the best calculation to number about nine millions. If, then, the Two Tribes number nine millions, how many ought we to expect the Ten Tribes to number? If the Two Tribes have stood and survived the shock and persecution of centuries when known, and therefore open to assault, is it not reasonable to suppose that the Ten Tribes will be in existence, a numerous and powerful people, for they have been hid, and thus have they evaded the persecution that a knowledge of their nationality would have entailed upon them from the Gentile and Pagan nations.

Some, indeed, persist in looking for God's chosen seed—His people, His inheritance—among the bushmen of Africa, the Indians of America; indeed, wherever they can find a people mean, and few, and very low in the scale of civilisation. They overlook the fact that Israel, not the Jews, were to be the most powerful and prolific people on the face of the earth, to be as sands of the sea, as the stars of heaven. Especially were these promises to be true in the latter day—for then God promises to multiply them, men, beasts, and the fruits of the field. This is one of the signs of the times, and it is a remarkable one. See our harvest, see our cattle, and see the Saxon race—doubling, at least, every forty years. No other nation is doubling at that rate. Germany comes the nearest, and both in Prussia and Austria they only double every one hundred years. In one hundred years from to-day the Saxons will control the world for peace and Christ.

To this end God is overturning, and will overturn until the whole world shall be federated around one throne, and that throne is David's—the only throne God ever directly established, and the only one He has promised perpetuity to. God has a land—Palestine. He has a people—Israel. He has a throne—David's, and for that throne He has a seed, just as the seed of Levi was selected for Temple service.

This kingdom is the fifth kingdom, to be set up in the latter days of those kings, says Daniel. The kingdom was never to be left unto other people. It is typified by the stone cut out of the mountain that is to fill the world. Why then stand amazed at the cession of Cyprus to England, if she be Israel? To her was promised the isles of the sea, the coasts of the earth, the waste and desolate places—the heathen and uttermost parts of the earth, as a possession. Already out of the fifty-one million square miles which composes the earth, England, including the United States, now owns about fourteen millions, or say one-fourth. She bears rule over one-third of the people of the earth; she adds a colony every four years on an average. At the present rate it will not be long before the kingdoms of this world will be given to the saints of the Most High. It is no marvel in the light and instruction of prophecy that this throne and people should be so stable and prosperous.

Turn your attention to the founding of this throne of David. You will find the throne and seed unconditionally federated, the place and measure of prosperity conditioned on the obedience of the people and throne of God. "The Lord has sworn in truth unto David; He will not turn from it; of *the fruit of thy body* will I set upon thy throne" (Psalm cxxxii. 11). Again "I have sworn unto David, thy seed I will *establish for ever*, and build up thy throne to *all* generations" (Psalm lxxxix. 3, 4). This promise is to all generations—not a part, nor simply for sixty years. For the kingdom was rent in twain when Rehoboam, the grandson of David, began to reign. The throne of David would be about the poorest type of Christ's throne and rule, and reign, if we can only see it in Palestine. There it was soon divided, very corrupt. "If ye can break My covenant of the day and night in their season, then may also My covenant be broken with David My servant, that he should not have a son to reign upon his throne. . . . . Thus saith the Lord: If My covenant be not with day and night, and if I have not appointed the ordinances of heaven and earth, then will I cast away the seed of Jacob and David My servant, so that I will not take any of *his seed* to be rulers over the seed of Abraham" (Jer. xxxiii. 25, 26). Let anybody of the same mind read the seventh chapter of the second book of Samuel, and they will see that God promised to David that his house and kingdom should be established for ever, and that God would set up the seed of David after him. Well might David exclaim when he sat before the Lord, "Who am I, O Lord God, and what is my house, that Thou hast brought me hitherto? And this was yet a small thing in Thy sight, O Lord God; but Thou hast spoken also of Thy *servant's house for a great while yet to come.*" It is a pity men will not take and interpret the Bible by the rules of common sense.

David at this time was king over all the Tribes and was at peace, and settled and prospered. But God told Him that "He would appoint a place for *My people Israel,* and will plant them that they may dwell in a place of their own and move no more." This promise was to Israel. If the promises of the multitudinous seed were to be fulfilled to Israel, then it would be necessary to find them another place, for Palestine wouldn't hold them. So God has planted them. God never promised to find the Jews another country; Palestine is specially reserved for them. They have been without country, king, or government. In the year 725 B.C. the Jews and Israelites were separated, and since that time they have never been united. But the day is coming, says the prophet, when they shall dwell

THE THRONE OF DAVID. 181

together and appoint one head over them. The Israelites are only to return to Palestine representatively (Jer. iii. 14).

When Nebuchadnezzar carried the Jews captive, he took the king, Zedekiah, with him, and destroyed all his family, and all the real royal seed of David. Zedekiah died in Babylon. He placed upon the throne of David Gedaliah. Now Gedaliah was not of the seed royal; but God was displeased and permitted the crown to go to others. Ezekiel was taken captive to Babylon in the reign of Jehoiachim, the father of Zedekiah. The prophecy of the text was written in Babylon, and refers to Zedekiah, whom Ezekiel calls the "wicked prince of Israel, whose day is come, iniquity shall have an end. Thus saith the Lord God, Remove the diadem and take off the crown, this shall not be the same; exalt him that is low, and abase him that is high. I will overturn, overturn, overturn it, and it shall be no more until He comes whose right it is; and I will give it to Him."

Now all this is plain if we keep in mind that Zedekiah was the last prince of the House of David that ever reigned in Palestine. God removed the diadem. But in the course of time a lawful heir of the seed of David shall appear, and the throne and the seed will be established again in Jerusalem. It is to this end Providence is overturning Turkey to make way for this seed royal. But where is this seed royal? Answer: It is on the English throne. Listen carefully to the following:

Jeremiah tells us that with him he had the daughters of Zedekiah, who had by some means escaped the destroying edicts of Nebuchadnezzar (Jer. xliii. 6). And from Jer. xliv. 14, we learn that they visited Egypt, and from Jer. xliv. 28, we learn that a small number escaped. Now Jeremiah, being the only prophet in Judah at that time, had a right to take charge of the royal seed. He could not stay in Egypt, nor in Palestine, nor would he go to Babylon. Where, then, did the prophet go? He no doubt took ship with the Danites, and sailed for Cornwall, in

England, for this place was called Tarshish. We learn from Ezekiel the ships of Dan traded in tin, and other things. History and tradition both agree that there landed on the coast of Ireland in the North, a divine man and a princess. God had promised to Jeremiah his life wherever he went. "But thy life will I give thee for a prey in all places whither thou goest" (Jer. xlv. 5).

The North of Ireland had been settled with the Tribe of Dan; they at once understood who their visitor was. They called him Olam Folla, meaning a divine man or teacher. The princess was called Tea Tephi, the beautiful one from the East. This princess was married to Heremon, of Ulster, the king of Lothair Croffin, for such was the name of the city of Tara. This word Tara is Arat spelled backward. The Hebrew reads from right to left; English left to right. Lothair Croffin was changed in Tara at the time of the wedding. Tara means

JACOB'S STONE.

law. Thus began the seed of David to take root, and from there it spread over all Ireland, then to Scotland, thence to England, and Jacob's Stone in Westminster Abbey marks the journey of David's throne, and has always kept with the seed, and they have been always crowned on it. Ezekiel's riddle is at once solved. The tender twigs were Zedekiah's daughters. One of these twigs was planted by the great waters in a land of traffic. Our Episcopalian friends intended by their beautiful service to aid the members of their communion to read in order, and through the Bible, or a given portion of each chapter, once per year. But strange to say, this 17th chapter of Ezekiel, they have left out both in the Old and New Lectionary. It is itself a riddle, why this should so happen, that the only two chapters of the Bible left out or precribed are the 17th and 21st of Ezekiel. Surely blindness in part has happened to Israel, and what we esteemed as accidental, in the increased light of Revelation, stands to view as the ordered purposes of an all-seeing God.

The royal standard of England has nine lions on it and a unicorn. Let anyone set this standard before him as a map, the right hand will represent East, the top, North; left, West; the bottom, South. The unicorn comes from the East, it has a chain round its neck. So the Tribe of Benjamin came that way, and, as Normans, were finally attached to the throne. The big lion comes from the West, so it did from Ireland to Scotland and London. On the top we have a crown, and on the top of this we have a lion. On the first quarter are three lions, second quarter one, on the third a stringed harp with an angel's head, and on the fourth, three lions; the total of lions nine, and a unicorn. The fact is, this standard, had we time, teaches a world of history, and with the Psalmist we may say: "Thou hast given a banner to them that fear Thee; that it may be displayed because of the truth" (Psalm lx. 4). The genealogy and descent of Queen Victoria from Zedekiah we will furnish you. This genealogy has been got up by the faithful and very persevering labours of the late Rev. F. R. A. Glover, M.A., and Rev. A. B. Grimaldi, M.A., two Episcopalian clergymen of England. The chart is supposed to be as near perfect as any such thing can be. If any of you find any defect be kind enough and let me know. In the following genealogy those who reigned have K. prefixed—the dates after private names refer to their birth and death, those after Sovereigns' names to their accession and death.

ADAM TO VICTORIA.

GENERATIONS.
1. Adam (B.C. 4000—3070), Eve.
2. Seth (B.C. 3873—2978).
3. Enos (B.C. 3765—2860).
4. Cainan (B.C. 3675—2765).
5. Mahalaleel (B.C. 3605—2710).
6. Jared (B.C. 3540—2578).
7. Enoch (B.C. 3378—3013).
8. Methuselah (B.C. 3313—2344).
9. Lamech (B.C. 3126—2344).
10. Noah (B.C. 2944—2006), Naamah.
11. Shem (B.C. 2442—2158).
12. Arphaxad (B.C. 2342—1904).
13. Salah (B.C. 2307—2126).
14. Heber (B.C. 2277—2187).
15. Peleg (B.C. 2243—2004).
16. Reu (B.C. 2213—2026).
17. Serug (B.C. 2181—2049).
18. Nahor (B.C. 2052—2003).
19. Terah (B.C. 2122—2083), Amthéta.
20. Abraham (B.C. 1992—1817), Sarah.
21. Isaac (B.C. 1896—1716), Rebekah.
22. Jacob (B.C. 1837—1690), Leah.
23. Judah (B.C. 1753), Tamar.
24. Hezron.
25. Aram.
26. Aminadab.
27. Naashon.
28. Salmon.
29. Boaz (B.C. 1312), Ruth.

GENERATIONS.
  30. Obed.
  31. Jesse.

KINGS OF ISRAEL.

  32. K. David (B.C. 1085—1015), Bathsheba.
  33. K. Solomon (B.C. 1033—975), Naamah.
  34. K. Rehoboam (B.C. b. 1016, d. 958), Maacah.
  35. K. Abijam (B.C. 958—955).
  36. K. Asa (B.C. 955—914), Azubah.
  37. K. Jehoshaphat (B.C. 914—889).
  38. Jehoram (B.C. 889—885), Athaliah.
  39. K. Ahaziah (B.C. 906—884), Zibiah.
  40. K. Joash (B.C. 885—839), Jehoaddan.
  41. K. Amaziah (B.C. b. 864, d. 810), Jecholiah.
  42. K. Uzziah (B.C. b. 826, d. 758), Jerushah.
  43. K. Jotham (B.C. b. 783, d. 742).
  44. K. Ahaz (B.C. b. 787, d. 726), Abi.
  45. K. Hezekiah (B.C. b. 751, d. 698), Hephzibah.
  46. K. Manasseh (B.C. b. 710, d. 643), Meshullemeth.
  47. K. Amon (B.C. b. 621, d. 641), Jedediah.
  48. K. Josiah (B.C. b. 649, d. 610), Hamutah.
  49. K. Zedekiah (B.C. 599—578).

KINGS OF IRELAND.

  50. K. Heremon fl. (B.C. 580). Q. T. Tephi. She was Zedekiah's daughter. Reigned 15 years.
  51. K. Irial Faidh (reigned 10 years).
  52. K. Eithriall (reigned 20 years).
  53. Follian.
  54. K. Tighernmas (reigned 50 years).
  55. Eanbotha.
  56. Smoirguil.
  57. K. Fiachadh Labhriane (reigned 24 years).
  58. K. Aongus Ollmuchaidh (reigned 27 years).

GENERATIONS.

59. Maoin.
60. K. Rotheachta (reigned 25 years).
61. Dein.
62. K. Siorna Saoghalach (reigned 21 years).
63. Oliolla Olchaoin.
64. K. Giallchadh (reigned 9 years).
65. K. Aodhain Glas (reigned 20 years).
66. K. Simeon Breac (reigned 6 years).
67. K. Muireadach Bolgrach (reigned 4 years).
68. K. Fiachadh Tolgrach (reigned 7 years).
69. K. Duach Laidhrach (reigned 10 years).
70. Eochaidh Buaigllcry.
71. K. Ugaine More the Great (reigned 30 years).
72. R. Cobhthach Coalbreag (reigned 30 years).
73. Meilage.
74. K. Jaran Gleofathach (reigned 7 years).
75. K. Conla Cruaidh Cealgach (reigned 4 years).
76. K. Oiloilla Caisfhiac'ach (reigned 25 years).
77. K. Eochaidh Foltlenthan (reigned 11 years).
78. K. Aongus Tuirmheach Teamharch (reigned 30 years).
79. K. Eana Aighneach (reigned 28 years).
80. Labhra Luirc.
81. Blathuchta.
82. Easamhuin Eamhna.
83. Roighnein Ruadh.
84. Finlogha.
85. Fian.
86. K. Eodchaidh Feidhlioch (reigned 12 years).
87. Fineamhnas.
88. K. Lughaidh Raidhdearg.
89. K. Criomhthan Niadhnar (reigned 16 years).
90. Fearaidhach Fion Feachtnuigh.
91. K. Fiachadh Fionoluidh (reigned 20 years).

THE THRONE OF DAVID. 187

GENERATIONS.

92. K. Tuathal Teachtmar (reigned 30 years).
93. K. Conn Ceadchathach (reigned 20 years).
94. K. Art Aonfhir (reigned 30 years).
95. K. Cormc Usada (reigned 40 years).
96. K. Caibre Liffeachair (reigned 27 years).
97. K. Fiachadh Steabthuine (reigned 30 years).
98. K. Muireadhach Tireach (reigned 30 years).
99. K. Eochaidh Moigmeodhin (reigned 7 years).
100. K. Nail of the Nine Hostages.
101. Eogan.
102. K. Murireadhach.
103. Earca.

KINGS OF ARGYLESHIRE.

104. K. Feargus More Mac Earca. (A.D. 487).
105. K. Dongard (d. 457).
106. K. Conrad (d. 535).
107. K. Aidan (d. 604).
108. K. Eugene IV. (d. 622).
109. K. Donald IV. (d. 650).
110. Dongard.
111. K. Eugene V. (d. A.D. 692).
112. Findan.
113. K. Eugene VII. (d. A.D. 721), Spondan.
114. K. Etfinus (d. A.D. 761), Fergina.
115. K. Achaius (d. A.D. 819), Fergusia.
116. K. Alpin (d. A.D. 834).

SOVEREIGNS OF SCOTLAND.

117. K. Kenneth II. (d. A.D. 854).
118. K. Constantin II. (d. A.D. 774).
119. K. Donald VI. (d. A.D. 903).
120. K. Malcolm I. (d. A.D. 958).
121. K. Kenneth III. (d. A.D. 994).

GENERATIONS.

122. K. Malcolm II. (d. A.D. 1003).
123. Beatrix m. Thane Albanach.
124. K. Dunkan I. (d. A.D. 1040).
125. K. Malcolm III. Canmore (A.D. 1055—1093), Margaret of England.
126. K. David I. (d. A.D. 1153), Maud of Northumberland.
127. Prince Henry (d. A.D. 1152), Adama of Surrey.
128. Earl David (d. A.D. 1219), Maud of Chester.
129. Isobel m. Robert Bruce III.
130. Robert Bruce IV. m. Isobel of Gloucester.
131. Robert Bruce V. m. Martha of Carrick.
132. King Robert I., Bruce (A.D. 1305—1329), Mary of Burke.
133. Margery Bruce m. Walter Stewart (I.).
134. K. Robert II. (d. A.D. 1390), Euphemia of Ross (d. A.D. 1376).
135. K. Robert III. (d. A.D. 1406), Arabella Drummond (d. A.D. 1401).
136. K. James I. (A.D. 1424—1437), Joan Beaufort.
137. K. James II. (d. A.D. 1360), Margaret of Gueldres (d. A.D. 1463).
138. K. James III. (d. A.D. 1488), Margaret of Denmark (d. A.D. 1484).
139. K. James IV. (d. A.D. 1543), Margaret of England (d. A.D. 1539).
140. K. James V. (d. A.D. 1542), Mary of Lorraine (d. A.D. 1560).
141. Q. Mary (d. A.D. 1587), Lord Henry Darnley.

SOVEREIGNS OF GREAT BRITAIN.

142. K. James VI. and I. (A.D. 1603—1625), Ann of Denmark.

THE THRONE OF DAVID.

GENERATIONS.

143. Princess Elizabeth (1596—1613), K. Frederick of Bohemia.

144. Princess Sophia m. Duke Ernest of Brunswick.

145.—K. George I. (1698—1727), Sophia Dorothea Zelle (1667—1726).

146. K. George II. (1727—1760), Princess Caroline of Anspach (1683—1737).

147. Prince Frederick of Wales (1707—1751), Princess Augusta of Saxe-Gotha.

148. K. George III. (1760—1830), Princess Sophia of Mecklenburgh Strelitz (1744—1818).

149. Duke Edward of Kent (1767—1820), Princess Victoria of Leiningen.

150. Q. Victoria (b. 1819, cr. 1838), Prince Albert of Saxe-Coburg.

Thus do we see how God has kept His word to David, and with this view, English and American history are at once understandable. The future is assuring and grand. God will assuredly overturn till His throne once more is planted in Jerusalem.

JEREMIAH AND ST. PATRICK.

Discourse XX.

The Prophet's Commission—His Life—The Tribes in His Day— Landing of Jeremiah in Ireland—What He Brought With Him—Colonisation of Ireland—Jeremiah the Founder of the Ancient Irish Government and Religion— Tea Tephi and Heremon—The Ancient Irish Flag—The Harp and Lion—Season of Ireland's Historical Prestige —Causes of Her Decline—St. Patrick a Benjaminite— How Rome Destroyed Jeremiah's Memory among the Irish —Destruction of Tara—Ulster Never Conquered—Irish Independence—Ark of the Covenant—Ruins of Tara.

" See, I have this day set thee over the nations and over the kingdoms, to root out, and to pull down, and to destroy, and to throw down, to build, and to plant."—Jer. i. 19.

IN these words we have set forth the divine commission given to the prophet Jeremiah. Never before, or since, was such a commission given to mortal man. It is not that Jeremiah is constituted a prophet for his own people, or over his own nation, and country, but he was divinely appointed and set over the nations and kingdoms of the earth, with an authority "to root out, pull down, destroy, and throw down." Surely he was rightly named, for the word Jeremiah means the exalted, or appointed one of the Lord. By common consent, the Jews gave him the first place and name among the prophets. Up to the time of the Babylonian captivity he was second, Isaiah being first. But after the captivity, on the re-arrangement of the holy canon, his name was put first, and ever after he was regarded and accepted as the patron saint of Judea. He was born of a priestly family, about 641 B.C., in the priestly town of Anathoth, which was situated a few miles North of Jerusalem, in the territory of Benjamin. His work and commission awaited him, because they antedated his birth, for he says (chap. i. 4), " Then the Word of the Lord came unto me, saying, Before I formed thee in the belly I knew thee; and before thou camest forth out of the womb I santified thee, and I ordained thee a *prophet unto the nations.*" Jeremiah's life-work, extent, and devotion, can only find a parallel in the majesty and compass of his commission. It is the extent of this commission that I wish you would specially notice, for it is neither tribal nor national in its limitations. He was ordained a prophet unto the nations. Hear the voice of his wailing (chapter xv. 10), " Woe is me, my mother, that thou hast borne me a man of strife and a man of contention to the *whole earth.*"

Consistent with the vastness of this commission is the recorded fact that he was forbidden to marry in his own land, for " The Word of the Lord came unto me, saying, Thou shalt not take thee a wife, neither shalt thou have sons and daughters in this place" (Jeremiah xvi. 2). The claims of a wife and cares of a family could only have been harshly fitted on to such a work and commission. Indeed, every peculiar fact in the life of Jeremiah may be best accounted for by taking into consideration the greatness of his commission. To discard this is simply to invite confusion, and yet, strange to say, many prefer confusion rather than admit that he performed the *rôle* assigned him of Heaven. For this very reason writers, even Jewish historians, are at a loss to account for the latter half of the prophet's life. They do not seem to know where he spent his last days; they know not the time, manner, nor place of his death. And why, you ask? We answer, Because they selfishly and persistently limited his life and labours to his own land. They have not been willing to allow that he was set as a prophet over nations and kingdoms. Then, again, they have been willing to allow him to be a puller down and a destroyer, but not a builder and planter. To grant that he was a builder and planter, would have obliged them to have found the place of his building and the objects of his planting. These they well knew could not be found in Palestine, and they were as loth as many are unwilling to-day to permit Jeremiah to leave his own land. A man who would be equal to the Bible must be large-hearted, generous, and free, not fettered and bound by the errors of youthful training, the selfishness of sectarianism, the bigotry of orthodoxy, or the indifference of infidelity, but seek the truth, no matter from whence, or what it upsets, or overturns of preconceived ideas. The command is, "Prove all things, and hold fast that which is good." To hear some people talk and lament, you would think that the command was, Prove nothing, but hold hard on to what you have got.

Try, now, and reasonably and patiently follow me while I trace the wanderings of Jeremiah in Old Ireland. You will be surprised to find how intimate Irishology and theology are.

Ireland and the Tribe of Dan have a peculiar history, which history can only be made plain by reference to the Bible. Ireland has had much to undergo, yet of it God says, "To the islands He will repay recompense: so shall they fear the Name of the Lord from the West."

Ireland's first name was Scuite's Land, or the Island of the Wanderers. Her second name was Scotia Major, and Scotland was Scotia Minor, and England was Tarshish, and Dannoii and Baratamac, or Land of Tin. Yar in Erin means the land of the setting sun. Hibernia is a Hebrew word, and means from beyond the river of waters.

Two colonies settled in Ireland; the first, the Phœnicians, who were the Philistines or ancient Canaanites; the second settlers were the Tuath de Danan, meaning the Tribe of Dan. The words are Hebrew, yet in Irish. For further information let any one read "Pinnock's Catechism on Ireland." The Phœnicians were a sea-faring people; pressed by Israel, Egypt, and Assyria, they finally left Canaan and settled in Ireland. We find nine-tenths of Irish historians agreeing on this. Then the monuments teach the same—ancient inscriptions, one of which written was, "We are Canaanites who have fled from Joshua, the son of Nun, the robber." The people who show tourists the seven churches of Glendenlough, say they are Hittites and Hivites. Again, ruins of Baal temples, Cromlechs, round towers, go to confirm the same. Customs—Baal fires, on May eve, in Irish Ninna-baal-tinne; funeral wakes, or cup of consolation, forbidden to Israel when they sought to copy after the Philistines. "Neither shall men give them the cup of consolation to drink for father or mother" (Jer. xvi. 7). The Irish language came from the Phœnician, the alphabet of both being composed of sixteen letters originally, the only alphabet in the world so agreeing. From the Irish came the Gaelic, Welch, Cornwall, and the Manx from them all.

The second settlement of Ireland is what puzzles historians of to-day—not the old historians, for they, nine out of ten, admit that the Formorians, Firbolgs, and Tuath de Danans, were one and the same people. They were a divine folk. The Tribe of Dan was a sea-faring Tribe, trading from Tyre to Tarshish for tin, and so became acquainted with the British Isles, and during Ahab's persecution many of them fled; so of the Simeonites who settled in Wales. This shows us why the North and South of Ireland should be so distinct to this day in religion, enterprise, and general characteristics. When the Tribe of Dan finally left Palestine, they with the other Nine Tribes went North, settling in Denmark, as in the North of Ireland, leaving their names on rivers, hills, cities, and things.

It is this that accounts for so many words of an Hebrew origin being found in the Irish language. General Vallancy has compared thousands and finds them thus related to the Hebrew. Instance: Jobhan-Moran, Chief Justice; Rectaire, Judge; Mur-Ollam, School of the Prophets; Ollam-Folla, Divine Teacher; Mergech, a Depository; Tara, Law; Tephi, Prince of the East; Lia-Fail, Stone of Destiny; Eden Gedoulah, Precious Stone.

If to Irish history we join Bible history, all is plain. God promised David repeatedly that he should always have his throne and on it his seed. The permanence of David's throne makes it a fit type of Christ's. Now, Jeremiah took charge of Zedekiah's daughter when Nebuchadnezzar took the Jews captive. He went to Egypt, then escaped, God promising to keep him whithersoever he went. So he disappears. No account of his death in the Bible. He had charge of the ark of the covenant, royal seed and Jacob's pillow—the stone of Israel. Irish histories, some twenty of which we find agree, say that about 585 B.C., a divine man landed in Ulster, having with him the king's daughter, a stone of destiny, and ark, and many other wonderful things. The people of Ulster, of Dan, understood the old adventurer. Jeremiah married Tephi, Zedekiah's daughter, to Eoiacaid, who agreed to abandon Baal worship and build a school for the prophets. So he did. He then assumed the title of Heremon of Tara. From Tara, which was changed from Lothair Croffin into Tara. From Tephi comes our goddess of Liberty, on old coins, sitting on a lion. Now, at Tara Jeremiah buried the ark of the covenant, tables of law, &c., and instituted the nine-arch degree of Masonry, to keep in mind its hiding-place—so all may understand Jer. iii. 16: "And it shall come to pass, when ye be multiplied and increased in the land, in those days, saith the Lord, they shall say no more. The ark of the covenant of the Lord; neither shall it come to mind; neither shall they remember it; neither shall they visit it; neither shall that be done any more." This means that when the ark is found the ceremony will end; for the ark has to be found and go before the Jews when they return to their own land. Jeremiah was the first Grand Master. He, too, is the real St. Patrick—simply the Patriarchal Saint, which became St. Patriarch, then St. Patrick. The Roman Church introduced St. Patrick to offset the St. Patriarch.

Jeremiah well knew where the Tribes of Israel were in his

day. He knew that Judah, Levi, and Benjamin were in Babylon, filling in the seventy years of captivity, and the small remnant that Nebuchadnezzar left of them in Judah were scattered hither and thither. The Nine Tribes, or Israel, were settled in Central Asia, and were spreading Northward and Westward. This he knew, as easily as Peter did centuries after, when he wrote his epistle to the brethren, scattered abroad in Pontus, Galatia, Cappadocia, and Asia; or as James, who dedicated his epistle to the Twelve Tribes which were scattered abroad; or as the blessed Master who commissioned and sent His disciples after the lost sheep of the House of Israel. The place and locality of the Nine Tribes were known to the Jewish nation in the time of Josephus, the historian, for he speaks of them, and gives them a fraternal letter which the House of Judah sent unto the House of Israel. You are to keep in mind that it is after this the Tribes of Israel are to be lost. All prophecies after 700 B.C., up to this, our day, and till about 1882 A.D., that had reference to Israel, plainly mark out the dwelling-place of these Tribes, and yet these prophecies, not being understood, till these latter days, Israel was as actually lost as if there had been no such prophecies. These prophecies were first sent North, then West, and then to the "isles of the sea." The law of the Gospel of Jesus would be sent to these Tribes; till then the "isles had to wait for the law." In due time this law was carried to them by the missionary Tribe of Benjamin. This very thing and time the prophet had foretold, for he says: "Wherefore glorify ye the Lord by the Urim; the name of the Lord God of Israel in the islands of the Western sea." How true, indeed, "the isles of the sea saw it and feared." Jeremiah knew that the Tribe of Dan were a seafaring people, and in their trading they had become acquainted with Northern Europe and the British Isles. During the persecutions of Ahab thousands of them had left Palestine, settling in Denmark—this word Denmark means the circle of Dan. In course of time they crossed the sea and took possession of the North of Ireland, settling in the province of Ulster. The Tribe of Simeon, that had ever cast its lot with Dan, left Palestine and settled in Wales. Read the prophetic benedictions of the Patriarch Jacob in the light of these historical facts, and they will stand out in sunlight brightness. "Dan shall judge his people as *one* of the Tribes of Israel." In his *oneness*, all alone he shall go out first, mark out and prepare the way of the other Tribes; and the royal seed, the ruling power, shall hide itself in him. "Dan shall be a serpent by the way, an adder in the path that biteth the horses' heel so that the rider shall fall backward." Yes, Dan will be hid among the Gentiles. He will bite them, sting them, frustrating their purposes. Then exclaims Jacob: "I have waited for Thy salvation, O Lord." Dan did wait, until the prophet Jeremiah landed in his midst with Tea Tephi, the daughter of Zedekiah, the royal seed, with the ark of the covenant, the tables of the law, the Urim and Thummim, which would enable Dan to judge his people, with the stone of Jacob, the pillar witness, which is now in the royal chair in Westminster Abbey; and also with the standard of Judah. Thus the prophet, who was the rightful custodian of all these things, carefully cared for the same, leaving them in charge of Dan. All but the stone have been concealed till the latter day. For on this stone have been crowned all the kings and queens of David's line.

Now just here we must take up history—especially Irish history—for in this matter and at this very point, you will find profane and sacred histories agreeing. One will beautifully explain the other; nor can anybody understand Irish history unless they get the key from sacred history. To take this key later writers have been unwilling, and, therefore, they have been unable to solve the problem embodied in this race and nation. No people on the face of the earth have been less understood and more misrepresented. The real allophyllians of

Ireland—that is, the first native settlers—are unknown. The present inhabitants are not autochthonal, no more than we are the first settlers of this country. On one point all historians are agreed—namely, that Ireland has been settled by two distinct colonies of people; and from these two colonies came the present Irish race. These two colonies were distinct in features, manners, customs, enterprise, and religion, and after all these centuries have passed away, these differences are discernable in some degree, especially so in enterprise and religion. And though, of course, in these latter years, they have become considerably mixed, yet an appeal on either of these points will mark out the Danite from the Phœnician. From the loud boasting of the Phœnician Irishman in Ireland, when speaking of America, you would think that he would pluck out his eyes and give them for a gift, if need be. Well, a few years ago, Chicago was bitterly scourged with a fire. The need and distress thus caused appealed to the nations of the earth for help. The response was grand and glorious. Even hateful old John Bull did well. But what did Ireland do? Take two of her leading cities as an example; one in the North, the other in the South. Belfast in the North, of the Tribe of Dan; Dublin in the South, of the Phœnicians. Belfast sent 36,000 dols.; Dublin, 2,000 dols. Why this difference? We answer, Forsooth, the people of Belfast are Danites; they of Dublin are Phœnicians.

The Phœnicians, or Philistines, were the ancient Canaanites. They took early possession of Ireland. On this point the old as well as the new historians generally agree. But there was another early settlement in the North of Ireland whom the historians called *Tuath de Danan*, which simply means the folks of the Tribe of Dan. They introduced into the Irish language hundreds of Hebrew words, with many customs and legends of the Hebrews. They were very distinct in their enterprise and religion from the other settlers. About the year 580 B.C. there appeared before this people a strange man, whom the historians call *Ollam-Folla*, which means a divine teacher; the name or title is in Hebrew. This man, whoever he was, soon wielded great power in their midst. What he commanded they seemed ready to do. He very soon inaugurated wonderful reforms. He gave them a parliament, made them give up their idolatrous customs. He founded a college to train students to teach and preach his religion. It was called *Mur-Ollam*, school of the Divine. Here, again, the name Hebrew, although in Irish. This wonderful man had with him a fair young princess, whose name in Hebrew-Irish was *Tea Tephi*, which means the beautiful one from the East. This lovely princess was married to the governor of Ulster, Heremon. He resided in the City of Lothair Croffin. In the agreement of the marriage, among many things, he was to accept her religion, give her joint authority, and build the Mur-Ollam, or college, and sustain it. Also to change the name of his city from *Lothair Croffin* to *Tara*, which means law; to adopt her standard or banner emblem, the harp and lion, and to be crowned on the wonderful stone called in Irish-Hebrew, *Lia-Fail*, which means stone of destiny sometimes called *Eben Gedoulah*, the precious stone. From this Tea Tephi, we get our female goddess of liberty, who on old coins is seated upon a lion with the Davidian harp in her hand.

Our text tells us that Jeremiah was to plant and build up. Here he planted, and here did he build. He planted and built a throne, a college, and a religion. Turn to Ezekiel, chapter xvi., and read the famous riddle. Tea Tephi is the tender twig that was cropped off from the high cedar, King Zedekiah, and planted among the merchants by great waters on the mountain of Israel. She was the tender one that was to take root downward. To Jeremiah, the Lord said, " Verily, it shall be well with thy remnant." Nay, more, He told him that He would give him his life for a prey, whithersoever he went. And in 2 Kings xix. 30, we read: " And the remnant that is escaped of the

House of Judah shall yet again take root downward, and bear fruit upward. For out of Jerusalem shall go forth a remnant and they that escape out of Mount Zion; the zeal of the Lord of hosts shall do this." And Ezekiel, in his captivity, sent forth a prophecy referring to the wicked prince, Zedekiah, saying of his throne in the name of Jehovah: "I will overturn, overturn, overturn it, and it shall be no more until He comes whose right it is, and I will give it Him." So was this throne overturned, and was never after established in Jerusalem. You will notice that there are three overturnings, and as Scriptural language is emphatic and not superfluous or tautological, these overturnings mean something. Turn to history, and you will find this throne has been turned over just three times—first, from Jerusalem to Ireland; second, through King Fergus to Scotland, and, third, through King James, from Scotland to England. This throne can never be turned over again, for Jerusalem will be incorporated into the British Empire. The throne has turned over till it got home again; hence, as surely as we live, Palestine will go into the hands of England. The throne, religion, and education established by the prophet have ever kept together. This is the secret of Ireland's prestige and marvellous pre-eminence in centuries past. The college of Armagh could boast of 7,000 students at a time. Missionaries went forth from Ireland through all Europe, teaching Christianity, and founding schools. Few men can compare to Virgilus, Eregina, Columbanus, and Columba. In olden times she was known as the "Isle of the Saints." The day of Ireland's weakness and distress came to her when she permitted her religion to be corrupted and controlled by foreigners; and by these same Italian intriguers she is now impoverished and enslaved. But for this the throne might have remained with her to-day, and England and Scotland have been under her. But when a nation loses her religion, she loses the right arm of power, and the ability to preserve freedom.

Jeremiah = Patron Saint of Judah.

200 THE LOST TEN TRIBES.

Jeremiah was the patron-saint for Ireland for a long time. Simeon (the Welsh) had and have David; and as surely as the Welsh have kept their saint, so surely ought Ireland. St. Patrick is looked upon by many as a mythical person. I believe, however, that he was a veritable man. The best authorities make out that he was born at Bonavena, in ancient Gaul, near what is now called Boulogne, some time about 387 A.D. He is reported as having died March 17th, 465, in the county Down. His father's name was Calpurnius. Young Calpurnius, or St. Patrick, as he was afterwards called, had a hard life of it in youth. I believe him to have been a Benjamite, a Christian; for the Benjamites began to fill in that part of France about that period. This tribe were by nature missionaries. This prompted him to desire to redeem his brethren in Ireland. In Ulster he began his labours. From this same Tribe others had visited Ireland. History mentions four who preceded St. Patrick. The name of St. Paul, by many, is connected with a visit to Ireland. It is very easy to see how Jeremiah, the patron-saint of Judah, would be installed in such a relation with the Danites after his death. He was the real sainted patriarch of Ireland, and by a crafty design of Rome, young Calpurnius was created sainted patriarch, or St. Patrick; and by this means Rome linked the greater part of the Irish nation on to herself. Anybody honest and familiar with history knows that St. Patrick was a Christian, and in no sense of the word a Roman Catholic. The fact is, Rome began early to covet Ireland. Once they got possession, it was necessary for them to destroy the influence of Jeremiah. This they did, in part, by substituting the name of St. Patrick in the place of the prophet's; and more, they then set to work to destroy even the old and famous capital city of Tara. In 565 St. Ruadham, along with a *posse* of bishops and chiefs of the South of Ireland, cursed the city, so that neither King nor Queen might ever rule or reign therein again. They forced the government, monarchy, and people to abandon the place. From thence Tara was deserted, and the harp sounded no more through Tara's halls. The city thus cursed crumbled to ruins, and remains to this day buried, awaiting a glorious resurrection. Rome caught her prize at last; but neither Rome or any other power ever enslaved or conquered Ulster. Beyond the pale—that is, the dividing line, running from the Boyne to the Shannon—Rome never got, nor never will. Irishmen clamour for independence, to be free from England, and wonder why they are not. The reason is that God cannot trust liberty to them; for a people that yoke themselves to a foreigner, and give themselves over to be governed in spiritual matters, would make a poor effort if trusted with their temporal government. We all know that if Ireland had been free, she would not long have remained so, for body, as well as soul, she would have committed to the Italians. Why Irish Catholics should ask for freedom when they so voluntarily bind themselves to a foreigner, I fail to see. As the Protestants of the North have asked, and had granted, spiritual freedom in the severance of Church and State, so let the men of the South ask and demand, and stop not short of freedom from Rome. A free religion is the parent of a free State, and a free State of free School. A people who are not wise enough to take care of their own religion, are very poorly prepared to be the guardians of liberty. My belief is that Ireland ought to be free. She ought to be an independent province, with responsible government, as other English provinces. And once she becomes free religiously, it will not be long before she will be free politically. Substitute Jeremiah for St. Patrick, and the Lord Jesus for the Pope, then the day of freedom will not long tarry.

In a recent sermon Dr. Wild said:—The agitation of Home Rule has not been conducted fairly. It has not been a free discussion; therefore the present result is not a proper sequence for us to judge; it is a sequence largely of terrorism, of murder, of agrarian outrages, of boycotting, and of intimidation. Many tradesmen and respectable citizens and landlords in Ireland are cowed to very silence. Who wants his house burned down? Who wants to have a bullet through his head? Who cares about sand-bagging, knocking him down? Who cares about his cattle being maimed in his fields? Who cares about his store being boycotted? Who wants to open his mouth, where to express sentiments would be to endanger his life? Can you get a fair expression from such a people? A plebiscite to-morrow in Ireland, if there should be no restraint, would vote to continue as they are, in my humble opinion. More; they have been helped by talk, and money and influence, from Britain, from Australia, from the United States, and from our own beloved Canada. Do you know, my friends, that the time may come when another party in Ireland may want just such help! If so, will they get it? For we have a fine precedent set us by this people. The Bond Street Pastor, in a year or two, may be out organising a league for the support of the loyal men in Ireland; and I would have just as good a cheek as Mr. Sutton to start one in Toronto. I would have as much courage to go all through this Dominion as he has, and I would raise money just as well as he has raised it. It is well for the people to know that this thing could be done, for it will save them from rashness, and it will be a help to them. Our very quietness encouraged them, and because we do not say much, excepting occasionally, they take our silence for cowardice, and our quietness for weakness, and think we could not do anything. We can do it when we want.

Foreign allegiance in things spiritual is always political insecurity at home, no matter what the church is—Congregational or Catholic—and we in Canada will not stand a church connected with the old country. Why should my Catholic friends have an allegiance to Italy, when we won't stand one in the Episcopalian Church, which has always been loyal; and yet we demanded a separation from the old country. The Methodists were forced to separate. Was there any reason? Well, we may say it is better. Well then, sir, if this is reasonable, I don't see why my Catholic friends want to have their head, and man who manages their spiritual business, as if they were so many little children, in Rome. They are incompetent priests, or they would be more successful. That is all. You have this illustrated in Bulgaria. Russia knew that the more she could propagate the Greek religion, the more hold she would have upon the people, and she soon upset Bulgaria against Turkey. You cannot have foreign allegiance in spiritual things without its being a weakness at home, and that is what some Governments and people do not seem to understand.

There have been wrongs done to Ireland—may be there are wrongs still existing. Let proper agitation and discussion, and proper presentation to the British Parliament be made, and the intelligence and willingness of that legislative body, I believe, would deal honourably with them. In time past the Catholic majority was so great and so hostile, that liberty had to be adjusted to that state of things. The potato famine broke that majority down very largely. They are little aware of the favours that the government has given them. In the centre of education, Maynooth College, two-thirds of the support has been from the British Parliament, by an annual grant, until, in 1871, they were bought off by the payment of 1,861,605 dollars. When, where, did a Catholic Government subsidise a Protestant College? They talk about our illiberality, yet the brilliant and most uncompromising enemies of Britain are the priests that are educated at Maynooth, who, without such aid, would still be in their brogans, and eating potatoes and buttermilk to-night.

Since the fifth century, when Roman missionaries first entered Ireland, there has been trouble from that day to this. There never passed by twenty-five years, since they got there, without there being some sort of rebellion in some part of that unhappy island. The people had a religion before a Roman missionary ever went there, and were pre-eminent for their learning—the Isle of the Saints. Once in power, they suppressed forethought, destroyed the great temple, palace, and city of Tara; transferred its influence and its gold to St. Peter's at Rome, and took the gold that covered the altar to burnish that in St. Peter's. They talk as if they had been there for ever. They talk about that being their own country. I challenge any Irishman or priest in Toronto to show me, from authentic records, that there was ever a Roman Catholic in that country before the fifth century. Now, they think they can do it. I am open for public criticism. If I miss a statement, I will catch it. They have no right to Ireland in their religion: it is a foreign religion. Ireland had a better one before it knew them, lived peaceably and prosperously before they came near the Isle, and would do so again if left alone.

Ireland's destiny is secured through the Tribe of Dan, which is one of the Tribes of Israel, who located in the North, and the Philistines located in the South and West. They were enemies thousands of years ago; they are enemies to-day. One is an idolatrous people, the others are pure in devotion; and for the Tribe of Dan's sake, Ireland will for ever be kept as a part of the British Empire. The Rev. Mr. Baxter makes Ireland free in the smash up of Britain in 1893. Ireland will be safe, for the simple reason, as he says, that she was not one of the ten-toed kingdoms of ancient Rome. She may not have been a toe; she has been a cat's-paw though, for many centuries, to rake in the money to Rome. Ireland in that department never had anything to spare, to tell the truth. He speaks of Britain as being one of the toes, and because she is, she will be crushed. No, no, Mr. Baxter, she will never be crushed. She is to live and enjoy the Millennium, and Ireland along with her!

Irishmen, especially my Catholic friends, find your best

friends in us. The very men you despise—Orangemen—are pledged to maintain your freedom. We have strong hands and stout hearts, and we are backed up by a religion that compels us to deal honestly, kindly, and fairly, without compulsion, to any man of any race or colour; so, whatever we say, we cannot do. you any harm. We cannot commit agrarian outrages. We cannot sand-bag you. We cannot fire a revolver at you. We cannot lift a hand against you, except in offices of kindness. Therefore, you that are here to-night, you can go home and be assured that, whatever I have said in myself, and in religion, I am obliged to be your friend in all that is essential, free and equal.

I hope sincerely the agitation in Ireland will come to a peaceable issue, without the shedding of blood, and that wise men and good men will see the real needs, and conform to the same; and may she have a recompense in the days to come, for the struggles she has passed through in years gone by. Peace be with Ireland. Amen.

PUBLISHED BY

ROBERT BANKS AND SON,
RACQUET COURT, FLEET ST., LONDON, E.C.
Complete Catalogue post free on application.

Talks for the Times. By JOSEPH WILD, M.A., D.D. Price 3s. Cloth, Bevelled Boards, Gilt Lettered. Sent by post on receipt of published price. 346 pp., crown 8vo.

CONTENTS.—Chapter 1. A Gift of One Hundred and Ninety-two Million Acres of Land. 2. The Return of the Jews to Palestine. 3. Folks that won't be Somebody. 4. The Four Prophecies of Egypt. 5. The Stone Kingdom and Dynamite; and the Orange Bill. 6. "144." 7. "666." 8. The Transit of Venus. 9. The Miracles of Antichrist; and the High Rock Image of Massachusetts, U.S. 10. The Man who could not sleep, and what came of it. 11. The Rainbow. 12. London Destroyed, and Jerusalem a Seaport. 13. Liberalism. 14. A Graft without a Stock. 15. Mouldy Bread and an Oath. 16. A Tombstone Inscription. 17. Dog Lappers. 18.—How to get Rich.

"Dr. Wild has an immense congregation. . . . We do not wonder, when we note Dr Wild's style, that he has such an enormous congregation of hearers. We wish we had a few such outspoken preachers on this side of the Atlantic. We recommend the book, and wish it a wide circulation."—*Philo-Israel in the "Banner of Israel."*

The Future of Israel and Judah. Being the Discourses on the Lost Ten Tribes, from "How and When the World will End." By the Rev. JOSEPH WILD, D.D. With Portrait of the Author. Containing Chapters on the Jews—Time of Christian Unity—"Thy Will be Done"—Weights and Measures—Just Weights and Measures—Ark of the Covenant—The Ark and Masonry—Jacob's Pillow—"The Corner—Manasseh and Communism—Identification and the Rev. Henry Ward Beecher—King, People, and God One. Price 2s., post free 2s. 3d., cloth, gilt, printed on toned paper.

"We are glad to find Dr. Wild has published a fresh collection of his sermons on the subject which interests him and ourselves so greatly. It has been brought out in excellent style, and we recommend most strongly that all our friends should obtain the book. Once in their hands, we know they will read it to the end, as we have just done ourselves. There are many most valuable points which Dr. Wild brings out in his present work."—*Extract from Review in the "Banner of Israel."*

A Message to the Church from the Nineteenth Century. By the Right Rev. BISHOP TITCOMB, D.D. Second and cheap edition. Crown 8vo., cloth boards, 1s. 6d.; sent free for Postal Order.

The Coronation Stone ; and England's Interest. In It By Mrs. G. ALBERT ROGERS, Author of the "Folded Lamb," "The Shepherd King, &c. With an Introduction by the late Rev. G. A. ROGERS, M.A. Fifth edition. Price 1s. 6d., post free 1s. 8d.

Fifty Reasons Why the Anglo-Saxons are Israelites of the Lost Tribes of the House of Israel. By. Rev. W. H. POOLE, D.D. Price 6d., post free 7d. 64 Demy 8vo. pages in wrapper. One dozen copies sent free for a Post Office Order for 6s. The best pamphlet to place in the hands of a person unacquainted with the subject.

Who Are We? and What is Our Mission? By J. THORNHILL HARRISON, of Ealing. With Seven Maps, printed by the Woodbury Permanent Process, illustrating—

1. Showing the Dispersion of the Family of Noah after the Flood. 2. Great Western and Eastern Plains. 3. Colonization of the Tribes of Dan and Asher from Phœnicia, B.C. 1400 740. 4. The Assyrian Empire, B.C. 710. 5. Extent of the Persian Empire and its Division into Twenty Satrapies, B.C. 521 to 464. 6. The Parthian Empire, B.C. 207 to A.D. 226. 7. The World with the Commencement of the Christian Era.

The work is printed on good toned paper, and handsomely bound in cloth, bevelled boards, with handsome design in gilt on cover, gilt lettered. Price 5s., free by post for postal Order.

"Every page betrays the pen of a thoughtful, able, and earnest writer—a man thoroughly acquainted with the literature of the subject from the Bible downwards, and imbued with a deep sense of the truth of Biblical prophecy."—*Bedfordshire Standard*

Anglo-Israel Tracts. 8 pp. Royal 16mo., on toned paper. Adapted to enclose in letters, and for general distribution. No. 1.—The Case Put Precisely. By the Right Rev. BISHOP TITCOMB, D.D. 2.—The Inheritance of the Gentiles in Israel. By PHILO-ISRAEL. 3.—Why Accept Anglo-Israelism? By W. S. CAVILL. 4.—My People, and Sons of the Living God. By DOUGLAS A. ONSLOW. 5.—Our National Heirloom. By Mrs. G. ALBERT ROGERS. 6.—Infidelity; and Our Responsibility as Anglo-Israelites. By A E. I., Author of "The New Old Story." 7.—An Appeal to the House of Judah. By the Right Rev. BISHOP TITCOMB, D.D. 8.—The Crucial Test of Our Identity. By PHILO-ISRAEL. 9.—Some Common Objections and Misapprehensions. By Surgeon-General J. M. GRANT, M.D. 10.—Consistency. By DOUGLAS A. ONSLOW, J.P. 11.—The Times and the Seasons. By the Rev. ROBT. DOUGLAS. 12.—An Elementary Lesson on Our Identity. By Rev. C. W. HICKSON. Price ½d. each; 1s. 6d. per 100. 12 copies post free 6½d.

The Sisters of Harrowdale Rectory. A Tale of Great Interest for Young People on the Identity of Lost Israel, with a splendid double-page frontispiece, illustrating Harrowdale Rectory and Church. This book will be read by both young and old with the greatest interest By Mrs. M. A. SEARSON. Price 2s. 6d., post free 2s. 9d.; handsome cloth, gilt, bevelled boards. Suitable for presentation.

"In this work, the leading arguments used in support of Our Identity are woven into a pleasing story, which is both interesting and instructive. The description of the rectory is a beautiful picture of the quiet sanctity and repose of an English Christian household, situated amid that charming pastoral scenery which has its grandest development in the Southern and Midland counties of England. It will prove entertaining to young and old, and should have a wide circulation."—*The Heir of the World.*

Present-Day Problems, and How Anglo-Israel Truth Explains and Solves Them. By V. M. COX, Author of "Ephraim-Israel, the Pivot Nation of Prophecy and History." Price 3d., post free 3½d.; 3s. doz., post free.

Contents:—Our Identity with is Mission.—Imperial Federation.—The Eastern Question.—Rev. Archibald G. Brown and the Eastern Question.—Disestablishment. —Sabbath Observance—Foreign Missions.—Our Relations with Judah.—Our Relations with Russia Egypt -The Unemployed.—Th Irish Problem.—*Cui Bono?*—A Remedy.

Ephraim-Israel, the Pivot Nation of Prophecy and History. By V. M. COX. 16 pages, Crown 8vo. 1d.; 100 copies, carriage paid, 6s. 6d. Fourth edition. Very useful pamphlet for distribution.

Cardinal Proofs that the British are the Lost Ten Tribes of Israel—The Abrahamic Covenant. By F. W. PHILLIPS, of Birmingham. With Two Chapters by PHILO-ISRAEL. Price 6d. post free 7d. Third Edition.

The British Nation Proved to be the Remnant of Israel, and the Representatives of the Lost Ten Tribes. By J. H. WELDON, J.P. Second edition, Demy 8vo., 66 pp., in tinted wrapper; price 6d., by post 7d.

WORKS BY PHILO-ISRAEL.

The Geography of the Gates. With Map and six full-page, and one double-page, Illustrations, printed on plate paper. 208 pages, in handsome cloth, gilt. Price 3s. 6d.; post free 3s. 10d.

An Elementary Digest or Sketch of the Chief Facts and Teachings of the Great Pyramid of Egypt. Adapted to the Unlearned and Unscientific. 56 pages. Price 4d.

Are the English People the Lost Ten Tribes of Israel? An Inquiry establishing the Identity of the British Nation with the Lost Ten Tribes. Price 4d.

Our Identity with the House of Israel. Price 4d. Reprinted from "Clifton Chronicle Letters."

Historical, Ethnic, and Philological Arguments in Proof of the British Identity with the Lost Ten Tribes of Israel, Clearly and Simply Stated. Price 2d.

The History of the House of Israel: How They were Lost, and How They were Found. Told for the Children. Price 6d., cloth 1s.; post free 7d. and 1s. 1d. Fifth Edition.

Our Identity: What it is Not; What it is; and Our Obligations To-day in Respect to It. Being a Lecture recently delivered in London by PHILO-ISRAEL, and published by special request. Price 2d.; a reduction for quantities.

A Resume of the Scriptural Argument, Proving the Identity of the British Race with the Lost Ten Tribes. Price 1d.; 6s. per 100, postage 6d.

⁂ MESSRS. ROBERT BANKS AND SON, *Printers, Publishers, etc., Racquet Court, Fleet Street, London, E.C., will forward Post Free to any address throughout the World a Copy of their Catalogue of Works on the Identity of the Anglo-Saxon Race with the Lost Ten Tribes of Israel, and the Great Pyramid.*

Printed in Great Britain
by Amazon